THE SOCIAL SONNETS

M.D. Petti

Copyright © 2025 by M.D. Petti and Bluebonnet Books, LLC.

All rights reserved.

eBook ISBN: 979-8-9938559-0-5
Paperback ISBN: 979-8-9938559-1-2
Hardcover ISBN: 979-8-9938559-2-9

No part of this publication may be reproduced, distributed, or transmitted in any form or by any means, including photocopying, recording, or other electronic or mechanical methods, without the prior written permission of the publisher, except as permitted by U.S. copyright law. For permission requests, contact bluebonnetbookspublishing@gmail.com.

Book Cover Art by Daniel de la Fe and Cover Design by Chelsea Schermerhorn

Edited by Chelsea Schermerhorn

First edition 2025

for Debby

Shakespeare wrote 154 sonnets.

I wrote more...

But who's counting?

In fairness, social media was my muse.

Foreword

In today's modern world, I cannot think of a more anachronistic love than writing Shakespearean sonnets. And yet, here they are...

I wrote my first sonnet many years ago, after I graduated from CCNY as an undergraduate with a "useless" Bachelor of Arts degree in English. In the months following graduation, I realized that teaching was not to be my career path, so I browsed the NY Times Help Wanted section (yes, the physical, hard copy version, since there was no "online" then) without much energy or passion to find something to do with myself for the rest of my life. I needed a paycheck and a purpose — and in that order! Even to me, Brooklyn-born and -bred, the cold, steely skyscrapers of Manhattan's Midtown seemed a landscape of daunting, insurmountable height to climb in order to find some sort of entry level job. Plus, I hated the claustrophobia of elevators! Eventually, I landed a couple of temporary administrative office jobs in Manhattan, and one of them did propel me to a steady career path into the private sector business world, in which I am now in the twilight of my current career.

But a funny thing happened to me a few years into my early, useful career: A rhythm — soft and steady and surprising — introduced itself into my head one lethargic day in the office. It had an insistent pulse like a heartbeat that demanded I put words to it. And the words did come! Before I knew it, I had written my first Shakespearean sonnet right there at my desk, and stared at it as though it were a rare gem of inspiration gifted to me from a powerful literary source outside my own myopic world — an escape, maybe, from that world, or a reminder that another existed as an inner voice to be released. I hid that first sonnet, first in my office desk drawer out of sight of co-workers and then on my way home from work in my shirt breast pocket, close to my heart — even shifting my work tie over it occasionally as though blanketing it from the harsh NYC subway elements — and frequently put my hand over it on the subway ride home, protecting it, cherishing it, making sure I was not hallucinating its existence.

But that fragile piece of paper with my first treasured sonnet on it made it home safely that day — so many years ago now — and I have been chasing the beauty and perfection of Shakespeare's 18th sonnet ("Shall I compare thee to a summer's day...) ever since.

I trust I will never reach it, for the chase is still on...

~

Contents

Foreword	5
One-Write Stands...	14
A Poet Warrior	15
A Woman's Spirit	16
Allison	17
Behind Your Beauty	18
Geraldine	19
He's Just A Man	20
How Wonderful You Are	21
I'd Die In Dennis	22
Kiss Me, Darling	23
The Lovelorn Knight	24
Memorial Day	25
Maryann	26
More To Me	27
My Heart and Yours	28
O, Happiness	29
On Listening To Dvořák's Romance (in F Minor)	30
Streetwalker's Sword of Solitude	31
The Bus Boy and Bobby	32
The Maiden and The Sea	33
This Place	34
Without You Here	35
Through Rose-Colored Verses...	36
Dear Angela	37
Far Lovelier Are You	38
For the Summertime	39
Fragile Flower	40
Good-Bye, Sweet Spring!	41
Heart and Mind: Carol's Sonnet	42
The Hearth of June	43
Homeless Is My Heart	44
I Love You More	45
I Miss You Still	46
My Special Friend	47

One to Keep	48
Sima's Sonnet	49
Spring In Bloom	50
Sonnet for Suzanne	51
The Fairest Flower	52
The Lonely Rose	53
The Silence	54
This Autumn Space	55
Naming Names...	56
For Janice	57
Could Spring Be Lovelier	58
Heart of Gold	59
I'd Give Up Summer	60
To Dream Of You	61
You're More January	62
For Jennifer	63
As Seasons Go	64
Evening Star	65
For JCW (I)	66
For JCW (II)	67
Love's Season	68
This Velvet Midnight	69
For Karen	70
By The Narrows	71
Karen	72
Karen's Song	73
For Louise	74
Fool My Heart	75
I've Nothing More	76
Louise	77
Perhaps, A Kiss?	78
Upon This Dawn	79
Winter Kiss	80
You Always Shine	81
Your Lasting Glow	82
For Paula	83
A Beacon To My Eyes	84
Paula's Sonnet	85

For Mayra	86
Near Shepard Hall	87
One Heartbeat More	88
Remember, Mayra	89
For Rhonda	90
Infinity	91
Rhonda	92
The Apple of My Eye	93
For Sharon	94
Eternity	95
You'll Stay June	96
Sharon's Spring	97
Spring Love	98
Starry-Eyed	99
The Starlight of Your Gaze	100
The Taste of You	101
Within Your Eyes	102
For Sherien	103
Santorini Summer (Sherien I)	104
Behold the Summer (Sherien II)	105
Each New Year (Sherien III)	106
Summer's Soon To Be (Sherien IV)	107
Summer's Start (Sherien V)	108
I Seek You (Sherien VI)	109
Summer, Stolen (Sherien VII)	110
The Fairest Woman (Sherien VIII)	111
Gentle Goddess (Sherien IX)	112
Exotic Woman - (Sherien X)	113
Your Poet Warrior - (Sherien XI)	114
Upon Your Olive Cheeks - (Sherien XII)	115
A Love To Find - (Sherien XIII)	116
What Passion More? - (Sherien XIV)	117
Sherien's Greek Lover - (Sherien XV)	118
Holding Hands - (Sherien XVI)	119
For Stephanie	120
Because...	121
How Near to You	122
One Sweet Kiss	123

That One Time	124
Without Your Love	125
You'd Kiss Me Well	126
Your Shine	128
For Susan	129
Come Back To Me	130
Susan	131
Moon Moments...	132
How Would I Love You?	133
I Loved You Once	134
Iris	135
Leah	136
Lori's Light	137
My Constant Moon	138
Reby's Sonnet	139
Such Beauty, Born	140
The Chance	141
The Velvet Void	142
Why Look Upon The Moon?	143
Winter, Spring, Summer, Fall...	144
Winter	145
December, Deep	146
December's Coldest Day	147
I Ask December	148
I Dreamt of August	149
I Looked For Summer	150
She's More December	151
Within December	152
In January	153
A Break From February	154
I'll Miss the Winter	155
Spring	156
Allaire	157
Behold The Spring	158
Don't Leave Yet, Spring	159
My Favorite Flower	160
Once the Spring...	161
The Spring Snuck In	162

For Mayra ... 86
   Near Shepard Hall ... 87
   One Heartbeat More ... 88
   Remember, Mayra ... 89
For Rhonda ... 90
   Infinity ... 91
   Rhonda ... 92
   The Apple of My Eye ... 93
For Sharon ... 94
   Eternity ... 95
   You'll Stay June ... 96
   Sharon's Spring ... 97
   Spring Love ... 98
   Starry-Eyed ... 99
   The Starlight of Your Gaze ... 100
   The Taste of You ... 101
   Within Your Eyes ... 102
For Sherien ... 103
   Santorini Summer (Sherien I) ... 104
   Behold the Summer (Sherien II) ... 105
   Each New Year (Sherien III) ... 106
   Summer's Soon To Be (Sherien IV) ... 107
   Summer's Start (Sherien V) ... 108
   I Seek You (Sherien VI) ... 109
   Summer, Stolen (Sherien VII) ... 110
   The Fairest Woman (Sherien VIII) ... 111
   Gentle Goddess (Sherien IX) ... 112
   Exotic Woman - (Sherien X) ... 113
   Your Poet Warrior - (Sherien XI) ... 114
   Upon Your Olive Cheeks - (Sherien XII) ... 115
   A Love To Find - (Sherien XIII) ... 116
   What Passion More? - (Sherien XIV) ... 117
   Sherien's Greek Lover - (Sherien XV) ... 118
   Holding Hands - (Sherien XVI) ... 119
For Stephanie ... 120
   Because... ... 121
   How Near to You ... 122
   One Sweet Kiss ... 123

That One Time	124
Without Your Love	125
You'd Kiss Me Well	126
Your Shine	128
For Susan	129
Come Back To Me	130
Susan	131
Moon Moments...	132
How Would I Love You?	133
I Loved You Once	134
Iris	135
Leah	136
Lori's Light	137
My Constant Moon	138
Reby's Sonnet	139
Such Beauty, Born	140
The Chance	141
The Velvet Void	142
Why Look Upon The Moon?	143
Winter, Spring, Summer, Fall...	144
Winter	145
December, Deep	146
December's Coldest Day	147
I Ask December	148
I Dreamt of August	149
I Looked For Summer	150
She's More December	151
Within December	152
In January	153
A Break From February	154
I'll Miss the Winter	155
Spring	156
Allaire	157
Behold The Spring	158
Don't Leave Yet, Spring	159
My Favorite Flower	160
Once the Spring...	161
The Spring Snuck In	162

Woman of Spring	163
Summer	164
Common Ground	165
How Soon July	166
I Miss the Moon	167
I Miss You, August	168
I Search For August	169
Like Sun Through Summer Skies	170
September's Shore	171
Summer Solitude	172
Summer's Edge	173
The Gliding Gulls	174
The Naked Sun	175
The Summer, Lost	176
Fall	177
All Love Is Gold	178
Autumn's Heart	179
Fall's Good-bye	180
September's Beauty	181
Then September Came	182
There's No More August	183
We All Do Fade	184
A Sonnet For All Seasons	185
Each Day Its Autumn Meets	186
I Stand Alone	187
Summer Waves	188
The Longer Shore	189
Your Sweet Addiction	190
Be My Valentine…	191
No Love But Yours	192
Of All the Hearts	193
Upon This Day	194
Valentine Gift	195
Valentine's Season	196
What Is A Valentine?	197
What Love But You	198
For Our Only Son…	199
My Son, Beyond (I)	200

I Lost My Son (II)	201
Our Fathers (III)	202
Good Sons (IV)	203
Sunday Night (V)	204
Good Night, Sweet Son (VI)	205
Spring's Green Joy (VII)	206
Unknown Tears (VIII)	207
His Eternity (IX)	208
Beyond Your Death (X)	209
You're Gone, My Son (XI)	210
Your Father First (XII)	211
You Died Too Soon (XIII)	212
The Sycamore (XIV)	213
Just The Sky (XV)	214
Sanctum (XVI)	215
My Penance (XVIII)	217
The Sycamores (XIX)	218
We Search For Summer (XX)	219
Dust and Destiny (XXI)	220
Sunday At St. Charles (XXII)	221
Before My Sun Must Set (XXIII)	222
December's Joy (XXIV)	223
Months…	224
January	225
February	226
March	227
April	228
May	229
June	230
July	231
August	232
September	233
October	234
November	235
December	236
For My Wife, My Only One…	237
A Million Years Ago (I)	238
The You I Had (II)	239

The Best Bouquet (III)	240
It's Been Two Months (IV)	241
Whenever Night Prevails (V)	242
What Spring Is There? (VI)	243
I Hear Your Whisper (VII)	244
We Danced But Once (VIII)	245
August Dream (IX)	246
Widower Warrior (X)	247
Back To Berlin (OH) (XI)	248
Her Final Gift...	249
Little Gifts (XII)	250
About The Author	252

One-Write Stands...

A Poet Warrior

A poet warrior on static grass
begins to bare his soul to those drawn near.
His words beyond these few someday will pass,
to touch so many more, who soon will hear.

An unfamiliar mic is held too tight;
his voice is strangely amplified, not loud.
With nervous dignity, his lips recite
such dreams and passions to the patient crowd.

Within a man, his heart may skip a beat,
but courage fills the space like rushing sound.
His poem done, his purpose is complete:
to brave the silent howl and stand his ground.

Yet as he cedes his spot, there is a pause;
and then the summer sky fills with applause.

~

A Woman's Spirit

A woman's spirit shines within her eyes,
which gaze upon the world with special sight,
the kind that pierces through the darkest skies
to help find heaven when there is no light.

A woman's love begins within her heart,
but well beyond her gentle breast will beat
like midnight's starry pulses, spread apart,
then gathered up for morning's golden heat.

A woman's beauty, like no other, turns
my eyes upon you, while my heart will race.
You're all I need; through you, my spirit yearns
and finds its Heaven in your lovely face.

A woman's life gives life beyond her own,
but yours is given as my gift alone.

~

Allison

Dear Allison, I have no words to say
that could bring your child back to be with you.
I've no new knowledge of God's unknown play,
whose curtain falls before the last act's through.

But I can see a mother's loss reveal
an emptiness that fills her broken heart.
Your life goes on, yet you'll forever feel
you are an actress in another part.

I know that loss, that pain, that moves your soul
to question Why? O Why, He'd take my own?
There's no true understudy for your role;
there's only me to let you know I've known…

And only this, — that Time, in time, gives pause
to hear your heartbeat echo life's applause.

~

Behind Your Beauty

Behind your beauty beats a heart of gold
that moves me every time you're near to me,
and when you're not, I feel it beat as bold;
then, mine beats back in rhythmic poetry.

My heart beats with your heart. Through every word,
its thump-thump writes its love on every line.
You read this verse and thump-thump I have heard
your heart returning thump-thump's back to mine.

Thump-thump, another word that you have read.
Thump-thump, thump-thump, another line, complete.
Without a single spoken word, we've said:
Thump-thump, thump-thump, it's time our two hearts meet.

Theresa, each who reads our love, confessed,
will feel their hearts thump-thump within their breast.

~

Geraldine

Your beauty's richer than the summer skies,
whose icy blue is pale compared to you;
whose sun's a shadow to my gazing eyes,
while yours possess a light, both bold and new.

I pause upon the landscape of your skin,
more soft and vivid than a summer field;
and, captivated, know my heart within
has found a warmer vista you've revealed.

But in your smile, your beauty really shines,
and not because it's radiant to see;
nor for its luster, lifting up these lines —
but knowing your smile's only meant for me.

And, Geraldine, not even this can shed
true light upon your beauty, once it's read.

~

He's Just A Man

He's just a man, but we imbue in him
an idealism we cannot achieve;
and cheer him, on a balcony, in trim
of purest white so we may still believe...

that Heaven is a place of softest cloud
that floats above the sinful dirt of home.
And as his dove-like hand waves to the crowd,
he blesses all who've made the trip to Rome.

But well beyond this enclave, he'll inspire
a faith that global goodness will prevail.
What choice is there for us? — the devil's fire
consumes the world if he is left to fail.

And knowing men have raised him to this perch,
he'll die one day, but we'll become his church.

~

How Wonderful You Are

How wonderful you are, dear Nellie, young
with energy and beauty both to spare,
deserving of a sonnet's rapture, sung
to your sweet charms to which no one's compare.

And yet beyond your eyes of tender light;
beyond your lips, set soft, and soft your face;
your hair like strands of Heaven weaved from night
that darns the dark in lustrous wisps of grace...

Beyond your bright and loveliest detail,
I see, within, a girlish spirit, grown;
and gazing at you, I, a humble male,
must marvel at the woman I am shown.

The fault is mine and not men's eyes, dear Nell,
if this has failed to move men's hearts as well.

~

I'd Die In Dennis

I'd die in Dennis if I had my way,
and wait until the rhythmic, swelling tide
came back to carry me through Cape Cod Bay,
beyond this beach, where horseshoe crabs reside.

Or better, let me live for one more dusk,
its rosy pearl hatched from an oyster sky;
breathe in the salty air and ocean musk,
the shore embalming me before I die.

But should I somehow make it through the night,
I'll float above the silty sand at morn
with golden seagulls, tinged by dawn's sweet light,
who sing out I'm alive! with Heaven's horn.

Come join me then, this beauty's not for one;
it will not die when our own lives are done.

~

Kiss Me, Darling

Your lips were made to be devoured so —
their ruby honey flowing past my own —
Alas, your kisses I have yet to know
except, imagined, in each sonnet shown.

The silk and satin surface of your skin,
if touched would touch me deeply in my heart.
The way it wraps about your cheek and chin —
I feel it only in this softest art.

And from your eyes, a light has followed me
beyond real life, beyond these lines I write,
beyond what is of us and what should be,
into each dream I dream of you at night.

So, kiss me, darling; darling, kiss me, do...
Beyond this dream, how I have wanted you.

~

The Lovelorn Knight

Again, dear lady, here I am to place
not brick or stone or monument in gold.
God only knows why I fill up this space,
endeavoring these inky lines to hold.

Love, O love, — is it not in a word?
It is a gift I gild for all to view;
and crafted with a care most find absurd:
a poet's alchemy, penned just for you.

While other men pursue their maidens, fair,
and build them castles, fill their wombs with seed,
this lovelorn knight will write of love's despair,
erecting nothing more than this to read.

Reject my love, dear lady, raze my heart.
Shred not this timeless page and tender art!

~

Memorial Day

In expectation of true bravery,
we send young soldiers out for freedom's fights
with crisp, new uniforms and dignity,
and polished guns with locked and loaded sights.

Our backyard barbecues are stoked with pride;
each weekend warrior attends its flame.
Across the sea, perhaps a hero's died
too far from home; the public knows no name.

And mother cries good-bye as guests must leave;
while father mumbles, nursing several beers.
Old Glory hangs too still beneath their eave,
and can't distract each parent's hidden fears.

While both have played their patriotic parts;
the battlefield remains within their hearts.

~

Maryann

Your sweet, familiar countenance restores
my heart to childhood innocence and joy,
when Brooklyn blocks were distant lands; their shores —
the curbs we couldn't cross as girl and boy.

And yet the thrill of such a pretty face,
unknown to me in that close neighborhood,
defied the boundaries set by time and place,
and left me dreaming where I stared and stood.

But, now, grown-up and you, a woman, we
move well beyond the gridlocked lines of old;
for beauty knows no blocks in poetry,
and dreams of you I knew, anew unfold.

And though I can't love you like any man,
in this I love you more, dear Maryann.

~

More To Me

Your cheeks mean more to me than to his lips
that kissed them once, then not a second time...
more than his unkind touch by fingertips,
while mine caress you ever in this rhyme.

Your eyes shine more for me than he can see,
for blind to your love's sun, his world is night;
yet I, who gaze on you through poetry,
reflect their brilliance in each line I write.

And while he left you, I will always stay;
his heart had wandered, mine beats here in place.
None but a foolish man could turn away
from you, whose beauty turns me to your face.

You'll be remembered more by me in this
than by someone whose heart was more remiss.

~

My Heart and Yours

My heart and yours cruel distance cannot breach,
for there's no space between the love we share,
like stars that shine beyond our mortal reach,
yet light our wishes through the endless air...

Like miles that separate your touch from mine,
though you still touch me and still move me so;
and as my hand massages each new line,
you'll feel my pen's caress and tender flow...

Yes, I remember your sweet lips on me,
before necessity forced us apart,
before that moment became memory
to hold you here through this eternal art —

where my lips kiss you back in words that stay
upon this page that never goes away.

~

O, Happiness

O, happiness, elusive dove of dreams
that sun-ward soars on weary, scalded wings,
your light, as luminous as Heaven's, seems
to burn its shadow deep through all dark things.

Alight upon my life, dear dove, and stay,
for far too eager is your maiden flight;
then much too high are you, to my dismay;
then far too low when you have lost your height.

A beacon for my hopes, a wing and prayer,
a star that stays the course while others, lost,
fade out among the dark and dreamless air
like secret lovers, fled, their lives star-crossed.

Alight! dear dove, alight, and end your search, —
these lines your happy cage, my pen your perch.

~

On Listening To Dvořák's Romance (in F Minor)

Each breathless string, a voice that raises me
above the earth in concert with the sky, —
where lifted, I can hear what I can see
and, cloud-like, watch each violin fly by.

A solo strain amid these angels leads,
and carries me beyond both space and time, —
as if God summoned it for what He needs
to soothe my soul through each vibrato's climb.

Humanity, your poetry's aloft,
as horsehair bows and catgut lines align.
Mortality's transcended; death's made soft...
and fools me into thinking I'm divine.

Upon this reverie where I am blessed,
my heart is stilled but never laid to rest.

~

Streetwalker's Sword of Solitude

A warrior in urban wilderness:
she's armed with nothing but her wits and words;
ignores her beauty as though it were less
a weapon to display to hungry herds.

Amid the stubble-steel of unkempt streets,
she courses concrete, knowing love's pretend.
The bravest men — her challenged stare defeats —
retreat to shadows as their hearts descend.

But on each street, she walks with truth and light, —
her sword of solitude has slain her fears.
She's overcome her loneliness and fright,
to conquer feelings that once brought her tears.

My stare is not with voyeuristic eyes,
but with a poet's gaze her heart denies.

~

The Bus Boy and Bobby

His final question just before he died,
before the shock set in as millions stared,
before, again, that year a country cried,
was ...everyone okay? — because he cared.

The bus boy, Mexican and seventeen,
the last to shake his hand while still alive,
became a man amid that mortal scene,
and cradled him as though he should survive.

Despite the prayers and rosary, God's call
to Bobby put to rest his run that day.
The bus boy, witnessing this great man's fall,
had held him up in such a gentle way.

While history reveals its "truth" through years,
one man recalls it through his heart and tears.

~

The Maiden and The Sea

The sea spread out before the maiden's arms
would not reveal its secrets easily;
but she was equal in her will and charms,
and both their beauties captivated me.

The sea, both strong and free, with every wave
implores the maiden with its urgent hand
to join her sister on a quest to save
one lonely soul across one distant land.

The maiden sighs and then retreats ashore,
beyond the salty fingers on this beach.
She'll search alone and she must search some more,
her questions chasing her outside its reach.

And I will walk without her by my side,
my heart embraced by twilight's lowest tide.

~

This Place

The few, unwise, who once had run this place,
who preached the standards of what's right and wrong,
would not have recognized their own disgrace,
to look on younger men, not then as strong.

True strength lies in our faith when trust's betrayed,
beyond a church's pew or high school wall.
It lay in He, Who openly afraid,
faced death yet sacrificed His life for all.

So, men, remember that our Savior, Lord,
had worn a crown of thorns that men designed.
His blood and pain became His victor's sword,
His love of man the war He left behind.

And ours will be the noblest hearts each year, —
true heroes, marching on, against all fear.

~

Without You Here

Perhaps, there's nothing here of life or love;
and what I write is not true poetry.
What poet hangs his hopes in clouds above,
to force a rhyme for gaudy gallantry?

What dreams I've dreamed are not my own to keep —
they're borrowed wisps of midnight's sleepy light.
What loves I've loved are this romantic's leap
from messy beds to sheets stained virgin white.

And yet...your heart still beats with mine in this;
it skips a few and by the couplet's end,
I give you love's illusion and a kiss
so we'll be one, though we are merely penned.

Each time you read, I dare you not to feel
that words are life and this love's not for real.

~

Through Rose-Colored Verses...

Dear Angela

Dear Angela, each lily that I see
is not as bright and cheerful as your smile;
nor could a field of springtime flowers be,
whose blossoms spread across each sunny mile.

A rose in June could never feel as soft
as your sweet soul that Heaven holds today.
God called to you to be with Him aloft,
but what He took from us He took away...

Now, when we walk each day without you here,
upon a path through farm or city street,
we'll think of you through every month and year
until the time when once again we'll meet.

Our dearest friend, our friendship from the start
was meant to bloom and fill each other's heart.

~

Far Lovelier Are You

My love, far lovelier, more flowery,
are you than any rose, so red, I read
upon this page of tended poetry
that withers not nor dies in wilder weed.

More velvet is your skin, more soft your face,
more soaked in summer sun your sultry smile;
more intimate and fragrant your embrace
when holding you each brief, enduring while.

So, what does one more rosy than a rose
receive from her one love when roses pale?
My love, there's only one true gift that grows
beyond the time when thorny roses fail...

It's this, my love, it's this, for this will do
what roses can't for such a rose as you.

~

For the Summertime

One more sweet sonnet for the summertime,
one more before the voice of windy fall
will mock a poet's leaves of rusty rhyme
with autumn's hardy laugh and chilly gall.

One more sweet sonnet on this lonely beach,
where once too many people also lay.
We hardly noticed them within our reach,
or how July and August slipped away.

One more sweet sonnet for each rose that grew
for lovers' hearts and hands in early June.
From summer's garden, I picked one for you,
who let it dry and wither much too soon.

Upon this page, those petals found their floor,
as I write of the summer; then, no more.

Fragile Flower

Upon this untouched bed of spring I lie
and stare above into the pristine blue.
Then, caught between a chuckle and a cry,
at once I'm high and low to think of you.

I'd meet you shamelessly upon this field,
and taste the pleasure of your kiss again,
if you'd return without regret to yield
your naked lips to me, as you did then.

But April turned to May and May to June,
and June's new rose succumbed to too much heat.
Spring's fragile flower disappeared too soon,
like secret lovers, who no longer meet.

Though sun and blossoms fill the spring's sweet day,
my heart grows emptier where we once lay.

~

Good-Bye, Sweet Spring!

Good-bye, sweet spring, your daffodils have bloomed
and spent the April sun on their display.
How could they know their golden smile was doomed
to finally frown before the end of May?

Look at the early summer rose of June
whose petals, perfumed, velvety, and red
seduce our senses through July, though soon
the end of summer will pronounce them dead.

And what of you, sweet flower of my heart,
whose skin's more soft and smile's more filled with sun?
Will your true beauty wither and depart
or stay with me when summer, too, is done?

Your blossom, here, remains both read and gold,
untouched by fleeting seasons' heartless hold.

~

Heart and Mind: Carol's Sonnet

An artist's mind adorns a woman's heart,
like God adorns the springtime sky with sun,
whose beating, golden rays are Heaven's art
that gives good light on earth to everyone.

Below the gilded air, the meadows tune
to sacred sparrow song from lofty limbs.
Each daffodil of April, rose of June,
then lifts its petaled ears to hear their hymns.

And I, dear Carol, carol your sweet song;
tune my ink's rhythms to your lovely frame;
upon this page's canvas, sing along —
this "art," inspired by your art and name.

Your heart and mind create their artistry;
my pen and page their humblest flattery.

~

The Hearth of June

Behold this rose upon the hearth of June,
a ruby fire fallen from the sky;
its perfumed flame's extinguished all too soon;
its tender, velvet flesh is all but dry.

And like an ember shadowed by despair,
this darling, scarlet bloom of nature lies
upon the ground and seems beyond repair,
until your hand, my love, gives it a rise.

It breathes again upon your breath's inhale;
its blush renews as your lips kiss its head.
What once lay dying now sees life prevail,
for love will resurrect a heart, thought dead.

No summer will deny a rose its due;
my heart cannot deny my rose is you.

~

Homeless Is My Heart

Dear lady, what good is the grandest home
of wood and stone or tempered glass and steel?
Without you here with me, I'd rather roam
than dwell within the vacancy I feel.

What good's a hearth in winter when I'm cold,
for only you beside me warms me through?
And when its flames die down, what do I hold
but darkness and the chill of wanting you?

What good the garden in the spring to grow,
a rose to pick from early summer's blooms?
I'd never put it in a vase for show,
when emptier am I than all these rooms.

Now, homeless is my heart, for I reside
outside your arms, which once held me inside.

~

I Love You More

I love you more than any word I write
could thus express my heart through dullest rhyme.
You are my sun, my moon, my star, my light...
my universe without each tick of Time.

Your eyes are brighter than the summer's shine;
your cheek, much softer than June's velvet rose.
One gaze, one touch, from you — I'd leave this line
and fall into your arms in dream's repose.

In all this world, there is no one but you,
who moves me to this feeble page to say
how much you mean to me; yet, when I'm through,
I crumple it and throw it all away..

Instead, my lips are mute for you to hear,
but speak the loudest as I draw yours near.

~

I Miss You Still

I miss you, still, beyond each summer day,
whose living heat cannot replace your own;
and as the full moon sweeps the sun away
at night, I miss you while I lie alone.

Against my chest, I clutch the memory
of your soft skin like summer's fragile rose,
whose velvet I won't past this season see,
while yours within my heart and mind's eye grows.

And what beside your eyes can pierce the night,
whose summer stars turn dull and dim from view?
Compared to them there is no fairer light
and, thus, the Heaven's fairest fair is you.

Beyond each summer, summer will not end;
I miss you, still, as this love poem's penned.

~

My Special Friend

What season's color is my special friend...?
The golden sun upon the fields of spring
that brings new warmth and life at winter's end
to lift the heart of every living thing?

The yellow bonnets of the daffodil
or crimson velvet of the rose in June?
Your skin's as soft as them, yet softer still,
like summer green laid down for lovers soon.

Perhaps, most like the full moon's sleepless eye
that watches over us romantically,
and paints its silver lining in the sky
to light earth's dark and lonely canopy?

Beyond each spring and summer's hue are you,
who colors my life, my dear friend, — you do.

~

One to Keep

Had I one beauty of the spring to keep,
before the summer sun usurped the sky,
to burn the darling buds of May too deep
while June's hot breath pronounced that they would die.

Had I just one...the daffodil won't do;
it smiles too early and then cries too soon.
The dahlia spreads too thin, a flighty shrew.
The crocus whispers death beneath the moon.

Behold the rose, in velvet is it dressed;
its sultry perfume will not dissipate.
And when it withers and is laid to rest,
it stays with me despite its sorry fate.

As you, whose scent and scarlet mystery
had scorched my heart but left your rose in me.

~

Sima's Sonnet

Were I an artist who could paint my art
upon the canvas of a love confessed,
I'd paint a rose to represent my heart,
and tattoo it across your gentle breast.

I'd capture sunshine not in strokes of gold,
but run my fingers through your lustrous hair.
Resplendent scenes of summer seas sketch cold,
so to your sparkling eyes is drawn my stare.

Alas, unlike your brush, dear Sima, mine
is but a poet's pen of inky stains.
And yet your beauty shines through every line
and in each reader's memory remains.

No matter that this page is framed in flaw,
your timeless portrait here inspires awe.

~

Spring In Bloom

Your touch, like springtime sun, awakens me
and warms my skin to vanquish winter's chill.
I'm flush with April's golden energy
that gilds the smile on every daffodil.

I taste the season's rain upon your lips
that, thirsty like the petals of a rose,
first test spring's urge in tiny, timid sips,
then drink their fill as lust for living grows.

And when we pause, I gaze into your eyes,
then catch my breath and breathe in your perfume;
and suddenly, between impatient sighs,
I fall in love with you and soon resume.

The spring in bloom is earth's unbridled bliss,
and mine is knowing it through your sweet kiss.

~

Sonnet for Suzanne

So soft the center of your velvet cheek,
more blushing than the blushing rose, maroon,
whose fragile nature must the summer keep,
to warm its heart and hold it safe through June.

Without the increased warmth of day, so mild,
its blossomed face would never grow and thrive;
yet mid-July forsakes its favorite child
for younger flowers, eager to survive.

So, Suzanne, I will hold you in my heart —
a rose beyond the rose no wish can save.
Too quickly gone, its beauty from the start
gave more to me than all that summer gave.

You'll keep my season soft and velvety,
a rose, whose beauty keeps in poetry.

~

The Fairest Flower

The fairest flower in the flower bed
is you, my love, whose cheeks, more rosy, shame
each springtime petal, blossoming and red,
and known to me by any other name.

The sweetest summer is within your eyes,
which look upon me with their sultry gaze.
I need no other light to light my skies —
you are my full-moon nights; my sunny days.

And when the blues and greens of summer turn
to autumn gold and autumn gold is laid
to rest on winter's bed of white, I yearn
for you, whose beauty's hues will never fade.

A rose beyond a rose that seasons yield,
you'll never wither in this poet's field.

~

The Lonely Rose

What have I of you but this lonely rose
that, plucked from briefest stems, lies dormant still?
Its rich and velvet flesh no longer grows,
yet woos me with a distant, floral skill.

I fear to touch it, lest its petals fall;
or sniff too closely, should its sweet perfume
no longer carry fragrant June to all,
but rather reek a staler note of doom...

Why must this summer end before its start,
before the solstice sends its golden sun
to heat the center of each lover's heart,
yet freeze my own before its red could run?

Now here is love, reposed in frozen hue;
its beauty incomplete, its summer through.

~

The Silence

This silence soon invades my pen and ink,
although the summer's green and heat arrive,
to fill each leafy vein beyond its brink
with sparrows' blood and song, to feel alive.

And yet no tunes upon this page are pressed
when swift September chants the end is near.
Who sings for summer, for my words, once blessed,
were cursed since June's first roses did appear?

Among the leaves and trees and birds and sky,
there's not a single sound that moves my heart
except the echo of your sultry sigh
within my ear before my hand could start.

By then, you'd left and left without a word;
let autumn come for every leaf and bird.

~

This Autumn Space

I see your beauty in this autumn space
that clings to summer in September's trees.
Though soon October will their green replace
with crusty leaves that fall on every breeze.

I feel your lips in every sun-kissed cloud
that swells with golden heat, abed in blue;
yet when the twilight comes, the sky's a shroud
that dims each stolen dream I've had of you.

O, stay, my love, and leave the fall to flee
back to the distant hills from which it came...
Forget this chill that's come for you and me;
sweet summer will our foolish hearts reclaim.

And I'll pick up this leaf, now read and known,
and hold it for you like a rose, first grown.

~

Naming Names...

For Janice

Could Spring Be Lovelier

Could spring be lovelier than you in May,
who holds the sun within your limpid eyes;
whose warmth is warmer than each golden ray
that kisses Earth below from azure skies.

What bud could bloom and blossom more than you?
whose velvet cheek and tender smile both fill
its season more than each red rose will do
or yellow brilliance of each daffodil.

No dream of spring, eternal, holds my heart
more than the dream of holding you as mine;
and though the spring each year must soon depart,
your beauty stays with me in every line.

Thus, you, dear Janice, more than spring's sweet air,
are lovelier, — more spring than spring, more fair.

~

Heart of Gold

Dear Janice, could I gild in gold my heart,
suspend its final beat eternally,
remove it from my breast — I'd share its art
of truest love for all the world to see.

I'd steal the fire of the sun today,
the cooler candle of the moon tonight,
to highlight my heart's glorious display
and gladly gift the world its precious sight.

For what is true love but one's monument,
a golden idol even God prays to?
And is not true love love that's Heaven-sent?
And is not my true love my love for you?

Then, this, my love, is my true love you hold;
and in your hands still beats my heart of gold.

~

I'd Give Up Summer

I'd give up summer just to be with you,
for summer shines within your limpid eyes;
I'd never miss its brilliant, burning blue
when gazing at the fire of your skies.

I'd never miss the rose's velvet face
when touching your soft cheek, or, Janice, sin
in missing summer's warm and wet embrace,
since you're much hotter, held against my skin.

And when the surging tide consumes the shore,
while walking on some private beach we find,
I'd never miss the ocean's yearning roar —
your beauty pounds my heart with waves in kind.

Let summer leave me for much of the year,
for I'll not know it's gone each day you're near.

~

To Dream Of You

To dream of you, dear Janice, is to dream
of sun and light and everything that's fair,
of midnight's moon that sends its silvered beam
to highlight heaven in your soft, blond hair.

To kiss you, Janice, is to kiss the lips
of beauty's goddess, come to Earth to steal
my mortal heart, whose mortal heartbeat skips,
and leaves me breathless in their tender feel.

To love you Janice, is to love the sky,
whose crystal blue by day and pitch by night
is infinite beyond my mind and eye,
yet raises me to its immortal height...

Where you, dear Janice, in this reverie
of moon and sun and sky are all I see.

~

You're More January

Your love's more January than July —
more winter's startled sense than summer's start...
unlike the brazen sun that blinds my eye,
more like the shy moon's light that melts my heart.

More fleeting than the frost of early spring,
which soon will fade upon the season's morn;
yet in its wake on every limb will cling
the sweetest dew for life to be reborn.

Though on each branch and bough young leaves will grow
above each field and garden's flowered bed,
they'll bid farewell in autumn's fatal show
of red remains, while this remains re-read.

Your love, unlike July's last withered rose,
through January and beyond still grows...

~

For Jennifer

As Seasons Go

As seasons go, your spring becomes my fall;
your tree limbs bud, my leaves grow brown and dry.
My sun is crisp and blue but not so tall,
while yours ascends to make a summer sky.

Canola seas of gold are paradise;
and turquoise waves embrace your heated shore.
My world is full of cold and snow and ice,
where winter has a hold and holds me more.

But hearts cannot perceive each season's end,
nor know the start of yet another, turned.
For once in love, there's only love to send
and beauty in the landscapes we've discerned.

And though my winter comes, your summer's mine
and warms me, Jennifer, through every line.

~

Evening Star

I gaze upon you, Jennifer, as though
the night were emptied of its starry space,
for you are all the universe to know
and all its brilliant beauty to embrace.

Upon the bosom of this naked night,
my head is laid and finds its dreamy rest.
My lips, as well, find theirs by candlelight
upon the Heaven of your gentle breast.

And I will kiss you for eternity
with every wistful word and restless rhyme;
although not mine, you're mine in poetry
and I am yours, my love, throughout all time…

where you will be to others' hearts, afar,
more wished upon than any evening star.

~

For JCW (I)

If summer felt the heat I feel with you
then June would be too cold to bloom its rose,
and all of summer's greenery would blue
with sudden shivers as the season froze.

The sun at sunrise would not glow in gold;
at dusk, the gloaming's gloomy fires die.
No flame on Earth could daily burn as bold
as you, whose sultry eyes ignite July.

And after twilight's August embers chill,
the stars that should have risen, hot and white,
no longer pierce the dark nor evening fill,
for you have stolen Heaven's flame tonight.

And what was lost of summer's beauty, Jen,
is found in yours through my impassioned pen.

~

For JCW (II)

There's life and then there's death, and in between
there's you and me upon this lonely page, —
its bed is made so we'll be always seen,
where days lie still so we will never age.

The blushing blossom of your tender cheek
is at my fingertips each time I read.
Your lips are soft and in their softness speak
to me through softer lines these fingers freed...

And there's no other now we'll find but here,
no moment capturing our heartbeats best,
than every word whose syllable draws near, —
like measured whispers breathed upon your breast.

Sweet Jennifer, between this here and now,
such love remains in verse's timeless vow.

~

Love's Season

Suspend the summer, Jennifer, for you
are fairer than the summer's fairest flower,
whose petaled cheeks your own soft cheeks outdo
with velvet skin my hungry eyes devour.

~

Forget the Fall for Fall cannot display
a soul as colorful in any tree,
whose leaves from limbs by winter blow away,
while your sweet blush remains for me to see.

~

And even spring, — whose growth renews my heart,
as resurrected buds and blooms arise, —
cannot give rise to feelings you impart
when I look at you with my yearning eyes.

~

Ignore them all, but please pay mind to mine,
for my love's season stays in every line.

~

This Velvet Midnight

Desirous, I stroke your satin skin,
my fingers relishing its dreamy feel.
Within your arms, I know that I'm within
a world that Earth alone could not reveal.

As I caress the contours of your face,
explore the realness of your cheeks and lips,
with each angelic feature that I trace
with devilish hands, God licks my fingertips.

Then rise with me, sweet Jennifer, and fly
into this velvet midnight, let us dare.
The Moon's arousal streams upon your thigh
and yours and mine will scorch the starry air.

And when we land, I'll lie upon your breast,
the landscape of your beauty, Heaven-blessed.

~

For Karen

By The Narrows

I still remember you, your hair like flame
that set the Brooklyn sky above afire,
who caught my eye before I knew your name,
but I knew loveliness and know desire.

Beside the waters of that borough's shore,
your crimson waves out-flowed the Narrow's flow.
My heart, consumed by you, could beat no more,
and lay like driftwood in your heated tow.

And through the sea of years, Time waded, cold,
until this moment when, again, your face
arose like beauty's phoenix, new, not old,
from fate's spent ashes to this poem's place...

Where, here, in lines my heartbeats re-ignite, —
My rhyme, ablaze and sealed in words I write.

~

Karen

O, Karen, Karen, can I take your hand
and travel back in time, when once we knew
a day in which no more was ever planned
than watching dawn and sunset's rosy view.

And there amid my carefree play, what joy
in cherishing the cherry of your hair,
as though your very heart, to this young boy,
had spread its fire through the ruby air.

If I could hold again those days, which led
your path from mine and mine from that sweet age,
I'd run my fingers through your locks of red,
to feel your heart beat then, as on this page.

Now, all I have of you is read on white;
and all your strands now stroked are lines I write.

~

Karen's Song

Your name is music to my silent ear,
its sound is sweeter rolled upon my tongue.
You bring to me the taste of yesteryear,
each moment of our past a note once sung.

And if my fingers could run through your hair,
they'd wade within its wavy, ruby rise;
caress its sunset, stolen from the air;
be swept away in twilight's subdued sighs.

But then the moon would come to gleam anew,
and set my dreams afire as I slept.
Then, Karen, Karen, I would call to you,
your own lips answering in dreams you've kept.

Upon this page, our heartbeats find their way, —
their melodies once lost in yesterday.

~

For Louise

Fool My Heart

I fear, Louise, my love to write much more
would fool me into feeling that you're mine;
Through every word that's poorly penned I pour
my heart, and thus my heart's in every line.

From each new syllable exhales a sigh
that midnight's wistful recitations make,
and every quatrains' repetitions cry
a sad, collective voice for your heart's sake.

But, in the end, the crumpling of this verse
ought be the only sound you're meant to hear,
for words of love in poems I rehearse
should not be paged, but whispered in your ear.

What speaks of love on paper you unfold,
speaks not my love, whose breath remains untold.

~

I've Nothing More

I've nothing more, Louise, than my poor heart
to give to you to hold against your breast;
no more than that, and this: my lonely art,
whose beats are freed from deep within my chest.

I've only one last kiss for your red lips,
like one sweet word, repeated many times;
one more eternity before love slips
between the empty breaths of these few rhymes.

One last surrender to this verse's plea,
before we part for parts that we must play:
Remember that you still belong to me,
for on the stage of life, we'll fade away.

No more than all these lines have I to give,
and yet its script will last, our love will live.

~

Louise

O, Sun, your golden shadow blots the land,
for I have found a light more light than you.
And if she gazes on me, she'll command
my heart to glow within her limpid blue.

O, Moon, your waning crescent frowns tonight,
cannot upturn the evening's solitude;
yet her full lips remain as full and bright,
and kiss in glossy red my darker mood.

Somewhere...some silly stars will twinkle; she
outshines them all with eyes, closed fast asleep.
Yet sillier shine I in poetry
that 'neath her pillow's placed for her to keep.

Should these dull words of love your dreams displease,
time's stare will bring your light to light, Louise.

~

Perhaps, A Kiss?

Perhaps, a kiss upon your gentle face
would soon impress you to remember me,
or would you think of it quite out-of-place
from I, who writes this distant poetry?

Perhaps, the interlocking of our hands,
then mine placed on your breast to sense your heart,
would touch you more than these few lines' commands,
or less, for my heart beats through lonely art?

There is no question that true love resides
within love's ache if not within love's act,
and what I feel for you, Louise, still hides
if not in words than in the love I've lacked.

So, kiss me back and let your heart reveal
that true love's truest art for me is real.

~

Upon This Dawn

Upon this dawn, a day, brand new, will break;
and I'll forget the dreams I've dreamt before.
For what are dreams to me when I awake
to you, whose dreamy smile enthralls me more.

And I'll forget the Moon in virgin space
that many gaze upon in love-struck awe.
Compared to yours, it's but a blemished face
that I perceive as Heaven's ancient flaw.

And all the countless stars on which were cast
my lovelorn wishes for one love to be...
Not one could shine as true nor shine to last,
like you, whose eyes, aglow, now glow for me.

Forget the night, Louise, the night is done!
The morning's here, and here you are, my sun.

~

Winter Kiss

Each time I bask beneath the sun's sweet rays
that, golden, gleam upon the winter air,
I think of you, Louise, in warmest ways —
your limpid eyes, your smile, your lustered hair.

In every sun-drenched cloud that freely floats
in lofty azure skies, I take you in.
My spirit soars above my heart, devotes
its softest flight of words to your soft skin.

And to my ears, a whisper Heaven sends,
that captures through its kiss of wind-blown trees,
a sigh upon your lips whose sound ascends
beyond their limbs to lines I write with ease.

On every winter walk, you're seen and heard
in God's grand beauty and my humble word.

~

You Always Shine

If I could free the sun from summer skies,
then gift it to you as an orb to share
within the limpid windows of your eyes,
more glorious would be the summer air.

Awake at night, I'd snatch each shooting star
before its fleeting brilliance burned away;
and seal the evening in a crystal jar,
like fireflies we caught as kids at play.

But never would I steal the moon's full glow,
remove its softest hue, so heavenly.
I'd leave it there for gazing lovers, so
they'd witness how their love's own light should be.

For in my heart, Louise, you'll always shine,
and make the moon and stars and sun seem mine.

~

Your Lasting Glow

Because of your sweet beauty's lasting glow,
to match the limpid candles of your eyes,
I see no sun by day at dawn's dull show,
no stars by night in Heaven's dimmest rise.

The moon, too wan, now wanes at midnight's hour;
my fullest dreams extinguish while I sleep.
The lonely evening turns the rose's flower,
I picked, from rosy hues to blues, too deep.

And as each shedding petal's shadowed soul
is scattered on this empty bed, a breeze
of summer soothes this lovelorn heart you stole,
which beats in bursts to beckon you, Louise.

No sun, no stars, no moon could ever spark
a world that, without you, is ever dark.

~

For Paula

A Beacon To My Eyes

Your eyes are but a beacon to my own,
and shine right through their windows to my heart;
and what I've seen I've always seen alone,
but what I feel I've felt for you, apart.

You are a part of every dawn's new light, —
its fragile glow takes hold upon earth's rim,
like your sweet lips that kiss away the night,
engulfing me, whose day had once stayed dim.

And when that sun must set again, I gaze
not on its darkened edge, but in your eyes.
For though I must surrender splendored days,
I'll soon be lost within your moonlit skies.

Perhaps then, Paula, dreams will light your way,
to find me waiting for you, night...or day.

~

Paula's Sonnet

Your eyes are brightest on this darkest day,
when all the worried world ignores their shine.
Such beauty colors springtime's dulled display,
whose earth and sky somehow are in decline.

The grass should feel as fine and soft as you;
its taut terrain instead is brittle green.
Your lips declare my heart must soon pursue
the sweetest rain, not found in nature's scene.

Above my world the sun's a pallid sphere,
whose offering is wan and waning fast.
But yours is gold and will not disappear,
and bathes me in a light that's lit to last.

While in your slightest gaze my spring's re-sprung,
so in eternal lines my love's re-sung.

~

For Mayra

Near Shepard Hall

We met upon the grass near Shepard Hall,
before our class began at ten to ten.
We talked together on that day in fall.
I wondered when we'd meet to talk again.

We used our books for seats, but turned the page
of conversation to familiarize
ourselves with life at such an ideal age.
You liked my smile; I liked your pretty eyes.

Then, somewhere in the distance, time began, —
its campus bell blared out impatiently.
We feared we'd be too late, and so we ran.
I wished I'd kissed you before history.

Too many falls would fall since that one day, —
when we both fell in love, yet rushed away.

~

One Heartbeat More

My friend, so many years ago, when we
had met, what force prevailed beyond that day
to separate us, was it destiny,
or just two hearts that could not beat one way?

Yet if I laid my ear upon your breast,
to hear the tender echo of our past,
would I not think my own heart were suppressed
beneath your softness, where it now holds fast?

Although I'd not abandon this found place,
where time is measured in fond memories,
the world, dear Mayra, neither slows its pace
nor stills its clock for words of love like these.

Yet, still, I stole one tick of time; then steal
one heartbeat more for us, for all to feel.

~

Remember, Mayra

Had I the chance to chance my life once more,
return to days when days were full of you,
like summer sunlight on a sandy shore
that burned our feet 'til cooling waves broke through...

Like moon-glow silvering our tender skin
beneath youth's sky of endless dreams to be...
Had I that chance, would I again begin
the journey back to you, and you to me?

The fires of each memory grow fast,
they spark then catch from such a humble start;
but, once rekindled, they will blaze to last
with flames that rise and heat my torrid heart.

Remember, Mayra, love must take a chance
when feelings, fired up, make their advance.

~

For Rhonda

Infinity

Had I infinity with which to play,
beyond the normal span of human time,
I'd sacrifice it all for just a day
of loving you outside this meager rhyme.

Each word caressed upon this empty skin
cannot compare to touching your sweet face.
Eternity in ink cannot begin
to know your feel or tender lips replace.

And Rhonda writing you into my heart
would never do for long, I'd drop my pen,
abandon poetry — such lovely art —
to kiss you once...then kiss you once again.

Although these lines forever will be read,
I've loved you more in one night's dream instead.

~

Rhonda

I'm captivated by your glowing smile
and by the light that dances in your eyes.
Their beauty stills my heart a long, long while
and steals its beats as these soft words arise.

I've found no face that's lovelier than yours;
no cheek whose pristine blush would shame the spring;
no lips as wet and sweet, like sunlit shores,
whose sea and sand will kiss in summer's fling.

And, Rhonda, ready is my own new sun
that only you and your true love could shine
upon this twilight world, when day is done
and dusk's dim dreams are dreamed to make you mine.

At morn, I want my dawn forever burned:
my gaze upon you and your gaze returned.

~

The Apple of My Eye

The blooms upon the apple tree, like you
are sweet and young and tender to the eye.
Their vivid bouquet captivates my view;
their scarlet burns the springtime's bluest sky.

The ripeness of their skin, too soft to touch,
their rosy flesh beneath, too pure to eat...
And thus when Adam's weakness proved too much,
his paradise was felled in sad deceit.

But I shall not each pretty fruit bereave
by bringing to it death by mouth or mind;
and you, dear Rhonda, should not tempt, like Eve,
my heart for lines I line for all mankind...

Or, this, our garden, will forever spread
beyond our lives, — a love, forever read.

~

For Sharon

Eternity

If I could hold you once, I'd not think twice —
while feeling such soft warmth (I've yet to feel) —
to toss these timeless words and sacrifice
my verse's longing and long-lived appeal.

I'd not think twice to press against your breast,
my heart upon your heart, both beating, bound.
I'd leave my poetry to those impressed
with love found here but not true love yet found.

And while to others' eyes this shines your name,
mine closing on yours, close, to me shows more
than all the ink, run dry, to pen your fame
on all the pages crumpled to the floor.

Dear Sharon, should your eyes one day eye this,
eternity, not I, has kissed my kiss.

~

You'll Stay June

No beauty but your own to June compares,
whose eager sun and gentle rose reveal
a dazzling glow in early summer's airs,
a soft and velvet skin to touch and feel.

The fragrant wildflowers I find afield
try hard to catch my eye, my nose impress.
I'd pick them all for you, yet they'd not yield
one bunch to match your unmatched loveliness.

And what in Heaven's sphere could I observe
to capture June's romantic night anew?
No distant blot of star or full moon's curve
can hold a candle to the sight of you.

Dear Sharon, you're more June than June can be,
and you'll stay June when June's abandoned me.

~

Sharon's Spring

What would the touch of such a tender cheek
feel like against my lips, drawn near to you?
More soft is it than April's tulips, meek,
which blush and bloom when kissed each morn by dew.

What would my eyes, agaze, in your eyes see
beyond the limpid clarity they show?
More blue are they, more infinite and free,
than is the open sky to Earth below.

And how would I, when close, against your breast,
restrain my heart from beating wildly loud?
For truer is its voice of love, professed
to you, than Heaven's, blown through thunderous cloud.

Dear Sharon, what, but thoughts of you, could bring
an inspiration far more sweet than spring?

~

Spring Love

O, tell me, love, what song a heart could sing
to warm you as the winter ends its stay,
to welcome all the lovely days of spring
as do the birds whose song the sky will play?

Yes, tell me how one heart should sound to you...
its beats burst out the rhythm of your name?
Or Heaven calling out in rapture to
his mistress, Earth, with thunderous acclaim?

Then, tell me, Sharon, tell me, if you've heard
one note above the other notes you hear —
for my heart sings of spring through every word
and every word's a spring, sung loud and clear.

Although your own voice may not soon reply,
I hear your heart speak spring in each beat's sigh.

~

Starry-Eyed

Dear Sharon, only you defied my fate,
uplifted me, when time had not been kind.
For me, to love again seemed much too late,
since all my stars were crossed and misaligned.

And yet as constant as the North Star, you
were fixed upon my heart and mind at night.
By day, you were the sun that burned right through
to clear each cloud occluding love's lost light.

Now, I look upward and, enlightened, see
more than an empty sky where dreams once soared,
more than the Earth's ungodly canopy, —
for loving you, my Heaven's been restored.

If all the universe should fade away,
for you, my eyes would stare and starry stay.

~

The Starlight of Your Gaze

Your lips, dear Sharon, tempt me to dismiss
my vacant life for one that's filled with you.
The sultry softness of your tender kiss
is all I'd need this night to pull me through.

The full Moon's but a shadow of the Sun;
its lonely light sneaks through this window frame;
the Sun itself a coward, quite undone
by you, whose eyes outshine and shame its fame.

And in the dark glow of this empty room,
I hear you whisper to me; feel your breath.
Your touch reclaims my body from its tomb;
your heart my heart from still and certain death.

The starlight of your gaze awakens me:
it's all the universe I need to see.

~

The Taste of You

The taste of you, intoxicating, thrills
my tongue, as my pen leaves my lips to line
each fluid word that from this poet spills
as ink, — a merry drunkard dropping wine.

Upon this page, my vintage passion's poured,
for passionate am I in telling you,
that you're more beautiful and more adored
in this read verse than in some lover's view.

So, drink, dear Sharon, drink along with me!
Imbibe the essence of each word each day.
Since my glass holds you in eternity,
all, too, will savor your rich, red bouquet.

Upon the palates of our hearts you'll grow,
for beauty, sipped at first, shall freely flow.

~

Within Your Eyes

I gaze within your eyes and see a sea
that swirls me in its pristine undertow;
and pulls me deeper than I ought to be,
into its depths of limpid indigo...

Then soar a height whose heat's an azure fire,
where I'm consumed by blazing blue, and burned.
For Heaven's high, and yet I reach much higher
to fall for you so I can be returned.

And this is love, dear Sharon, true love's light,
the gods create to spark the seas and skies,
that men try foolishly to steal in flight,
that steals my heart with one look in your eyes.

My love is blind while my eyes gaze at you
and bring to light your beauty, here, to view.

~

For Sherien

Santorini Summer (Sherien I)

Should I explore the summer in your eyes
and plunge within their sultry depths to view
the Grecian isles below exotic skies
that lift my dreams while I fall fast for you?

And cheek to cheek, I'd feel your rising heat,
and lips on lips would taste your liquid sun,
as Santorini's surf would lick our feet
while we lie down upon its beach as one.

But ought I dare to venture to your heart,
not knowing where this trip would take my own?
Should I, Sherien? And should you, too, depart
to spend your summer in my heart, alone?

No paradise on Earth could quite compare
to what I found in you in just one stare.

~

Behold the Summer (Sherien II)

Behold the summer sun caress your skin;
its golden hand much bolder than my own
to touch such beauty from afar, yet in
my heart I've touched you many times, alone.

I watch the moon reveal its light to you
from shy and silver eyes, which seldom see
your own eyes gaze above — they always do.
How I wish that their gaze were meant for me.

And from the tiny stars beyond, what suns,
what moons, what earths with lovelorn lives lie there?
How many find their true love's own love runs
to starry reaches rather than reach near?

No brazen sun, no moon, so shy, Sherien,
can feel what I have felt, see what I've seen.

~

Each New Year (Sherien III)

Forgive me, February, I've delayed,
beyond December's final days, my heart
from knowing happiness through vows I made
to find Sherien by January's start.

Forgive me now that March, then April, looms,
to bring to lovers spring's redeeming rain.
Though May may gift them flowers, June its blooms,
I'll blossom into brokenhearted pain.

And through July and August's lovelorn heat,
I swear the threat of autumn chill can blow
in late September; thus, I'll warm my feet
for dreams October and November grow.

And, still, Sherien, through every month's demise,
each year, anew, renews that year's good-byes.

~

Summer's Soon To Be (Sherien IV)

Could you remove the winter from my heart,
undo the frozen crust of its regret
that lies like snow on earth's most tender part —
so hidden that it makes the past forget?

Could you uncloud each grayish day, increase
the sun for summer, lest the summer fail
to heat us as it did last year in Greece,
as we to each new sparkling isle would sail?

But mostly would you please return to me
before our sunny springtime's gone for good?
Look! Spring's arrived and summer's soon to be,
and I'd enjoy them if I truly could.

Without you, my heart's not the same, Sherien —
a season, cold and gray, once warm and green.

~

Summer's Start (Sherien V)

How warm the recollection of your face,
like summer's sweet arrival every June
that greets the spring and then will spring replace
with each full sun by day, by night each moon.

Upon the crescent of those lips...your smile
once lifted me beyond that moon and sun.
Though I cannot forget you left me, I'll
remember more when our love had begun:

The first day of the summer's just a day,
but to my heart it is the memory
of when you came to me, Sherien, to say
you love me, too, but should not stay with me.

With every summer since that summer's start,
my heart rejoices 'til you break my heart.

~

I Seek You (Sherien VI)

I seek you as I would the summer, passed,
its humid heart escaping eager fall,
which cast its chill upon our time too fast,
as summer slipped from us — sun, fun, and all.

I seek you underneath that Grecian moon,
which lit the languid land in diamond light;
and though our crystal beach had waned too soon,
it left me seeking you in dreams at night.

But when we parted, love did not; its feel
remained with me through autumn's numb advance;
through winter's frozen fields, its heat was real;
when spring broke ground, my heart broke with romance.

I seek you so, Sherien, and so I seek
a summer you and I, year-round, will keep.

~

Summer, Stolen (Sherien VII)

Are you my eyes on lands not seen, Sherien —
on sunny islands in a secret sea;
my skin laid on each silky beach, pristine,
whose hot and naked sand caresses me?

...my lips that kiss the sultry air; my tongue
that licks its salty aftertaste clean through;
my heart that makes believe true love stays young?
My heart that beats so faithfully, are you?

Are you my sorrow, too, for summer's flown
with my inconstant lover, who'll betray
my trust on distant shores I've never known,
where summer, stolen, steals her heart away?

If only my heart roamed so free and far,
I'd be with you, not wonder where you are.

~

The Fairest Woman (Sherien VIII)

The fairest woman I would ever know
is she who'd steal my heart one day in June;
and through each night, in dreams, her face would glow
to fill the void with summer's sweetest moon.

The fairest ocean spread before my feet
is that whose empty surf had sung Sherien
in every serenading wave that beat
then broke, retreating to the sea, unseen.

The fairest lover whom I'd ever had
had vanished when our time could not hold fast,
and whether what we shared was good or bad,
we'd search for it when summer, soon, had passed.

The fairest woman knows I love her more
than just one summer we spent by some shore.

~

Gentle Goddess (Sherien IX)

What touch above the touch mere men bestow
upon your form reforms their basest part?
For they'll not venture past your skin, to know
the gentle grace that lies within your heart...

Yes, they'll love only by their fingertips;
and, crude, not comprehend that beauty lies
beyond the intimation of your lips
or shy seduction of submissive sighs...

So, what touch touches you without their hands,
and touches me to touch you as I can?
This page, — and each who holds it understands
each word for you rewrites the heart of man.

Immortalized by one man's mortal verse,
Sherien, your beauty will not be your curse.

~

Exotic Woman - (Sherien X)

Exotic woman of the Middle East,
your face forsakes religion's worried veil
and feeds these pagan eyes its sacred feast
of captive beauty, freed, in such detail:

Your own eyes shine on our embittered dusk,
rekindle hope in me, a western man;
and drawing close to you, your skin's sweet musk
converts me more than Catholic censers can.

Did John deny his head to Salome',
who danced the dance that even God forgave?
Would I not lose my own to you today,
though knowing well my heart should well behave?

Then dance, Sherien, my faith forgives your hips,
renews itself upon your cherry lips.

Your Poet Warrior - (Sherien XI)

No, God would not each man or men deny
the opportunity to find His light,
so when I found you for the first time, I
discovered my religion at your sight.

Jerusalem could not re-gild its dome
in gold more golden than my heart is true;
sweet Bethlehem could not be home-sweet-home
to Him more than my arms are home to you.

No Crusade carried out, no Constantine,
no Kingdom come, or fear of Hell's dark fire
could win my constant faith like you, Sherien,
who gift this sacred verse, which you inspire.

This man, not led by prayer or Holy War,
found God then you — your poet warrior.

~

Upon Your Olive Cheeks - (Sherien XII)

Upon your olive cheeks, humanity
unmakes its bed and lays its seasoned soul.
I stare at you, Sherien, and only see
a beauty that belongs to mankind, whole.

For from the ruin of poor Palestine,
whose children wear the land's unholy scar,
still touched, you rose and came to me — not mine —
but to all hearts from that place, lost, afar.

But how did you surmount your nascent youth
amid their enmity and hopelessness,
to make your own way to salvation's truth —
that love, not holy hate, does God thus bless?

My lips pray softly on your cheeks; and soft
to He, Who sent you, send Amen aloft.

~

A Love To Find - (Sherien XIII)

If I could be your love, then love could be
a paradise upon the Cretan shore.
By day we'd lie and look upon the sea;
make love by night, awake, then look some more.

We'd set our sail and sail the eastern breadth
of ancient waters to your homeland's soil,
where modern martyrdom meets sacred death,
for men, in His name, make spilled blood their toil.

How could one God be God to each torn land,
whose single search for truth yields no one gain?
And yet, Sherien, we love and understand
our hearts hold Heaven without Heaven's pain.

So, be my love and we'll show all mankind
the love we found is still its love to find.

~

What Passion More? - (Sherien XIV)

What passion more than poetry can make
my unrequited heart make your heart feel
that each new word I write is yours to take
to heart, beyond this page's penned appeal?

Did Eve feed Adam only Bible lore,
or Cleopatra, Antony dismay?
Did Juliet her Romeo ignore?
Penelope, Odysseus betray?

The history of man and love is this:
a tale to tell of joy or wistful woe.
Sherien, make me immortal with the kiss
that sweetest Helen did not dare bestow.

To all who'll love these words, what tragedy —
our love was loved through only poetry.

~

Sherien's Greek Lover - (Sherien XV)

Sherien's Greek lover lies upon the beach,
his bed black sand by Santorini's sea;
and though he waits, carefree, beyond her reach,
she lies with him in splendored memory.

Last summer's end had forced her to depart,
a refugee of pleasure's sultry whim.
Through autumn, winter, and then spring, her heart
grew sore and wistful to return to him.

But wanton waters of the Cyclades
have stirred men's ancient passions to explore
their most romantic opportunities
throughout the year, like he upon his shore.

From New York City's coast, again she flies
to be with her "true" love, to his surprise.

~

Holding Hands - (Sherien XVI)

I dream of peace and love for you and me,
a peace that spreads to all the earthly lands,
a love that reaches to infinity
from hate's unholy hold to opened hands.

The world can change because of friendship's start —
a single smile for me from your sweet face
will make your beauty race within my heart,
then all the universe is mine to chase...

Our love is one not even time can shake;
a poet and his muse is truth, divine;
and men may try, but try in vain, to break
our bond through verse, dear friend from Palestine.

So, take my hand, Sherien, and dream away;
tomorrow's dreamers read us yesterday.

~

For Stephanie

Because...

Dear Stephanie, you're beautiful because...
beyond your lips of shimmering delight...
beyond your starry eyes that give me pause
as do celestial wonders late at night...

beyond the surface of your skin, more soft
than evening's landscape smoothed by moonlit beams
that midnight sends from Heaven's shores, aloft,
to soothe the Earth's terrain in silvered streams...

beyond comparisons to summer's sky...
beyond the romance of the Earth and Moon,
you're beautiful because you caught my eye
and eyes that catch my words will catch my swoon.

Then, hearts beyond my heart will all respond
and beat like mine until the Great Beyond.

~

How Near to You

No more a child to my aged heart, you are
a woman, grown on me through every year;
and though we'd never spent each day as far
apart, it seems you've never been as near...

How near the tenderness of your lips feel.
How near the softness of your satin skin;
and though I must imagine them for real,
how near the dream their touch will soon begin...

How near the constellation of your eyes:
how hot its light, engulfing me in flame.
How near infinity my true heart lies.
How near is Heaven when I write your name...

So, Stephanie, how near you'll always be
to me through this far-reaching poetry.

~

One Sweet Kiss

If I could hold you once before, too late,
too many years have sadly passed me by,
before my heart no longer seeks to sate
its yearning for your touch before I die...

before the desperate hours of each day
have turned too numb so that by night I sleep
and wake no more in fits and starts, but stay
as still as death, awaiting God's good keep...

Yes, holding you would bring back life to me,
would resurrect my heart to feel anew
the rush of true love's blood, dear Stephanie;
and I would taste your lips — I've wanted to.

Then, drawing back to catch my breath in sighs,
I'd lose it once again, held by your eyes.

~

That One Time

Why does your heart withhold its feelings still,
and keep love locked behind its beating cell —
a prisoner held fast against her will
that raps against the walls that hold her well?

Would one touch be the key to love's release?
One kiss upon your lips unlock your fire?
One gaze within your eyes make doubting cease, —
let loose the limpid flames of your desire?

O, look how I'm imprisoned too behind
the bars of this poor verse; yet only this
allows me to express my love in kind,
allows me that one touch and that one kiss.

Allow me that one time, dear Stephanie,
and love, once penned, will soon be love set free.

~

Without Your Love

Without your love, my love, what would I be?
A man who faces loneliness too long
forgets he has a heart, dear Stephanie,
until he feels it in his sonnet's song.

Until each word becomes its pulsing beats,
each line the veins that carry its desires,
which, coursing through the flesh of empty sheets,
takes on a life that only love inspires.

So, in your hands you hold my very heart;
and in your heart I hope you hold me too.
For though I've nothing but this humble art
to give, I give it lovingly to you.

All reading this through time, in time will hear
their own hearts' loneliness beat loud and clear.

~

You'd Kiss Me Well

Dear Stephanie, my lips would kiss you well,
and though you'd kiss me back reluctantly,
our sighs would sound, and they would surely tell
how much we both had wanted this to be.

My hands would reach behind to draw you in,
and press you close so there could be no space
between your heart and mine; and we'd begin
a soft surrender to this new embrace.

And just before a doubtful thought or two,
before your mind could overrule your heart,
I'd kiss you deeply and then deeply you
would kiss me so we we'd never be apart.

No, I would never let you go or miss
the chance to take a chance on that first kiss.

~

Your Eyes Are Bluer

Your eyes are bluer than the summer sky.
Your lips, more wet and full than seas, spread wide.
When caught within your gaze, I soar; then I
will plunge within your kiss's surging tide.

Your tongue is tastier than Eden's fruit.
Your breath, more scented than the springtime air;
and though the season's fairest flowers root,
the flower of your face still grows more fair.

Your beauty, Stephanie, is worlds apart
from earth's dull wonders; and more wonderfully,
you are the only world within my heart;
and more — you're all the universe to me.

Beyond my eyes, more eyes will see you, for
in this your beauty's shown forevermore.

~

Your Shine

How beautiful the sun within your hair;
it weaves a golden tapestry of light.
My fingers play with every strand; they dare
to hold each wisp of brilliance with delight.

The sparkling centers of your limpid eyes
do put to shame each galaxy afar —
as well, the full moon near; and, thus, the skies
all prove to me how lovelier you are.

Your shine outshines each day, your glow outglows
each night in which I, lonely, look above.
Each thought of you rethinks what Heaven shows
my heart, which searches for the truth of love.

The dreamy sight of you is all I see
and lights a world once dark, dear Stephanie.

~

For Susan

Come Back To Me

Come back to me, to me the years have passed
like petals, fallen off the summer rose,
that I had gathered and hold on to fast
within a heart, whose loneliness still grows.

Come back, for life's sweet bloom has dulled and dimmed,
when once eternal spring seemed green and new.
And love's illusion was so grandly trimmed
in endless sun and splendid thoughts of you.

No, never leave again, dear Susan, please —
for nothing's crueler than unsaid good-byes,
like silent breezes blown through autumn trees
that send once tender leaves to their demise.

To this uncertain leaf, my words succumb;
come back to me, so fall may never come.

~

Susan

O, Susan, softer than a summer day
of pillowed clouds upon a sky-blue bed
are you upon whose satin skin I lay
my lonely hands and then my weary head.

I feel your beating heart beneath your breast,
its calming rhythm warmly pulsing through
like sultry evenings when the Moon's undressed
and bares her silver charms for Earth to view.

And in this universe of distant skies,
where neither separate stars nor souls may meet,
it's in the locking of our yearning eyes
that God is real and we feel Heaven's heat.

All else beyond ourselves is dream or prayer, —
and only love can light the empty air.

~

MOON MOMENTS...

How Would I Love You?

How would I love you, could I love you more
than merely pressing you with feeble lips?
I'd soon command the ocean waves ashore,
to kiss you with their crests and drenching dips.

Then calm the surface of that twilit sea
so you could know the stillness of my heart,
between each scarlet beat that torments me,
before another pounding beat will start...

I'd steal the stars above, though they would fade.
Why snatch the Moon, it monthly loses light?
How would I love you, could a love be bade
to neither dim nor darken out of sight?

...through this, and only this, where time's defied,
each word a beacon through life's ebbing tide.

~

I Loved You Once

I loved you once, before this day and time,
when lines were uttered indecisively;
before there was a meter and a rhyme,
whose music gave my heart its melody.

I danced with you, although I cannot dance;
no rhythm found its way to two left feet.
And yet I'll waltz you with such fine romance
across this poem's floor where we can meet.

I dreamt of you through every lonely night,
my head upon the pillow of the Moon;
I'd close my eyes and suddenly take flight
beyond this space that daylight breaks too soon.

I loved you once, before my words could fill
this empty page to say...I love you still.

~

Iris

How could I write you when you write so well,
as though your own words are the world to you?
These lines I cast can never cast their spell
upon this page as brightly as yours do.

The stars glow silently upon their perch;
the Moon meanders mutely, lost in shine.
Like theirs, my voice is stifled, as in church
when God's epiphany booms down divine.

And still I write for you, dear Iris, I,
in stuttered syllables and rougher rhyme,
with pen, as dumb as me, because my eye
finds courage in your beauty every time.

So, please forgive this crude and bumbling art,
for when you read this you will read my heart.

~

Leah

A thousand flames are lit within your eyes
and kindle hearts with their resplendent glow,
as though your beauty can command the skies
and shame the sun, whose candle burns too low.

Your lips the oceans of the world would dry
and drown men's reason in their luscious swell.
The Moon's full countenance would wane and cry,
as poets find your face, then kiss and tell.

And even I, who've plumbed love's deepest seas,
have searched the heavens for inspired sight,
don't know the words to float on lines like these,
which fail to bring your loveliness to light.

Now, humbly on this page, I, Leah, lay
my pen, whose murky ink is swept away.

~

Lori's Light

I saw the stars within your eyes one night
and gathered them upon my own heart's sphere.
They shone in rhythm with such steady light
and made a galaxy for us appear.

I looked upon the Moon and found your face,
then dreamed of flying there to steal a kiss;
yet fearing lonely miles through empty space,
I sealed my lips and, thus, returned to this.

And only time will tell when love is real;
what galaxies still stir, what stars still fly;
whose heart stays broken and whose heart can heal...
Can yours, like mine, through words that never die?

And in this universe these lines create,
it's you, dear Lori, who decides its fate.

~

My Constant Moon

I see the Moon and then I see your eyes;
they search for me upon this distant place.
The stars stay silent, but I hear their cries,
and only time connects each empty space.

The tips of trees caress your silver skin.
Your face is kissed by clouds with wispy lips.
Yet, still, you look for me despite the sin
of human failing when devotion slips.

And faith? Yes, faith is in your lofty sight...
In you, whose heart has never missed a beat,
to sound a constant call to me at night
and guide me back to you from dark deceit.

If I could hold you as the Moon holds me,
you'd be the only light I'd ever see.

~

Reby's Sonnet

O, Reby, Reby, from a distance, we
adore you so, — pretend to know you well.
Your sultry beauty swoons this poetry, —
allows each lovelorn heart to kiss and tell.

Your smile's the crescent Moon above our eyes;
we gaze upon your lips of glossy light.
More than the flowing Moon in evening skies,
your hair's a lustrous stream of softest night.

And even in the morning, your sweet face
outshines the dawning Sun for all who wake
upon each day whose daylight can't replace
the dreamy sight of you, for Heaven's sake.

While God's own Sun still sets, His Moon still wanes,
your brilliant beauty in each heart remains.

~

Such Beauty, Born

Such beauty, born, belongs to every eye,
cannot be owned or selfishly possessed.
The Sun and Moon that grace our earthly sky
are no one's heat and light, and yet we're blessed.

I cannot stroke your golden strands of hair,
then hold your dawn within my parted palm;
or gaze within the silver of your stare,
in sweet surrender to the evening's calm.

Instead, you're with me in each lasting line,
reposed upon the pillow of my dreams;
this sheet, my bed; this love, much more divine
than flesh and blood conjoined in mortal schemes.

And, Jasmine, just as truest beauty's free,
your own belongs to none; but here, to me.

~

The Chance

Had I your tender lips before me now,
in muteness would my own confess my heart,
by uttering no word or single vow,
lest sighs are such when kissing lips do part.

Your eyes before me would my gaze command
and shift their focus from the day to night,
like twilight's fire o'er the setting land,
whose sun surrenders to the Moon's soft light.

But here, before me, still your beauty shines,
reflecting more than Moonlight's palest beam.
You radiate in these poetic lines,
whose chance to win you is my only dream.

Before me lies this page, its ink is cast
like shadows, where love's fleeting light has passed.

~

The Velvet Void

Imagine what the Moon had felt one day,
across the distance from his lover, Earth...
The velvet void between their bodies lay
like sinful space that punished both from birth.

In time, the Earth would glow with gravid sea;
the Moon spill silver through his sunlit tears.
He whispered to her despite gravity,
but all that answered was Earth's silent years.

Eventually, her children boldly crossed
the lonely miles to touch his pallid skin.
They searched for answers yet returned as lost,
and wondered, too, if they'd committed sin.

With every crescent phase, the Moon reveals
a smile for them, not what his heart conceals.

~

Why Look Upon The Moon?

Why look upon the Moon, whose light will wane,
to see the constant splendor of your face;
or stars whose timid shine will not remain
past dawn's disruption of such tender space?

Why gaze upon each cloud in beds of blue,
to see the glimmer in your limpid eyes?
For they, through rain, will grayer turn, not you,
whose tears of joy redeem those darker skies.

I look for beauty but your beauty gleams
beyond a fickle Moon or fragile star.
It shines for me and all the world, it seems,
and draws in hearts no matter where they are.

And you, whose heart is ever nearest mine,
become my universe through every line.

~

Winter, Spring, Summer, Fall...

Winter

December, Deep

The deep December in my lonely heart
cannot thaw out the frost of missing you;
where once you were its warm and sunny part,
prevailing emptiness now freezes through.

Your absence spreads like ice through all my veins,
and arms that once held you against my chest
embrace the cold, for only cold remains;
and love's remains have, too, been laid to rest.

Some tell me that the sun of summer soon
will once again return my heart to red;
but I'm more moved by winter's waning moon,
alone and pale in Heaven's darkened bed.

Dear Death, yes, cover me with winter's pall!
My heart forsakes the summer, spring, and fall.

~

December's Coldest Day

You held me once, my love, but would not hold
a heart whose tenderness was in decline,
like sunshine reaching through December's cold,
to grasp the needled frost upon the pine.

Your lips, that briefly found my frozen cheek,
like summer whispers kissing winter's face,
had sought to thaw me, but no longer seek
to waste their warmth where they feel out of place.

And as you let me go, this hardened land
embraced me closer than your closeness could:
the icy limbs of bony trees at hand;
the empty sky caressing brittle wood.

Good-bye, my love, December's coldest day
remained with me, but ushered you away.

~

I Ask December

I ask December nothing more than this —
restore these moments before winter's start:
the tenderness of springtime's virgin kiss,
the summer's golden touch upon my heart.

Restore the frozen ember of the sun
that fails to reach the zenith with its light.
And come the frigid moon when dusk is done,
restore its silver heat and sultry night.

Before the snow and ice lay claim to all
and shroud in somber stillness all I see,
at least suspend the winter for the fall, —
when death's delayed and colors every tree.

Or let December have its willful way,
so your love pulls me through each wintry day.

~

I Dreamt of August

I dreamt of August in the wintertime,
when every tree becomes a mannequin,
stands statuesque in bitter cold and rime, —
no coat of leaves conceals its skeleton.

The pounding waves upon the summer shore
restore the lonely beat within my heart.
My feet beneath the beach feel heat and more —
a love for living and a renewed start.

And yet each seashell stranded on the sand,
though beautiful, arriving with the tide,
reminds me winter's death is close at hand,
delivered from a place where none can hide.

How far from winter did my August seem;
yet still too close, for summer's but a dream.

~

I Looked For Summer

I looked for summer, but my winter came,
delivering its frost and icy blast.
It froze me in my tracks and staked its claim
upon a heart whose heartbeats fell too fast.

I searched for comfort in embracing arms,
but touched such brittle bark in every limb.
The sturdy sycamore, whose leaves were charms
for lark and light, now looms both bare and grim.

And where's the sun, whose lofty, golden gaze
once looked on us, whose love was summer-made?
It set your skin afire; eyes ablaze;
and banished winter to its distant shade.

I'll find a summer through each wintry day;
though summer leaves, our love will always stay.

~

She's More December

The distant sun within the winter sky
reminds me of the love that got away.
She's more December than she was July;
yet, still, her summer stays with me today.

I think she loved me once, but who can tell?
Too many dawns and dusks since circled past.
For time casts years and years their timeless spell —
her heart's more shadow now than light to last.

And see! God's struggling orb attempts to rise
above the spindly trees to help me search.
Too quickly does it drop, as though His eyes
find more eclipse than sight atop each birch.

New winters come and go, but never seem
to find a love more destiny than dream...

~

Within December

Within December, there's a hidden heart
that thaws the icy limbs of bony trees
and melts the snow that blankets winter's start,
whose solstice shrinks the sun and its degrees.

Although I gaze upon the frozen sky,
whose gray is cold like stone and still as death,
above the granite clouds, you catch my eye —
an angel, blue and bright and warm as breath.

And, yes, your constant love breathes life in me
as though the summer wind arrived this day,
exhaling winter's frigid memory
and whispering with warmth along the way.

Then, pressed against my breast to bring its beat,
your heart, uncovering the season's heat.

~

In January

In January, I endure the pain...
A winter much too warm; too gray its air.
Expected snow falls down as dirty rain,
like forced confession from unheeded prayer.

I walk upon this grass, too green, too wet;
too soft to hold the weight of life's retreat.
There's no one here but me and deep regret,
as deep as soil once dug beneath my feet.

Each year, I stand before this heavy stone,
whose polished granite will my face reflect.
And yet, your name's upon it — not my own;
unworthy, I still come to pay respect.

If I could take the fall, restore your years...
I'd welcome death and celebrate your tears.

~

A Break From February

A break from February's frigid feel,
although the sun's still limp upon the sky;
and yet, a taste to come that can't be real
of springtime warmth that I cannot deny.

A walk upon this road, both brittle, cold,
and coated in the season's morning frost,
slows down my steps as though they've grown too old,
and falling now would be the last line crossed.

Instead, I'm resurrected by your face,
your smile more golden than the silly sun
that feebly shines upon this frozen place,
yet finds the spring before the spring's begun.

And thus, my heart finds you in every beat;
my winter thaws before my frozen feet.

~

I'll Miss the Winter

I'll miss the winter when the winter goes
and takes with it the comfort of the cold
that spreads its blanket of repeated snows,
to warm my heart with virgin white and gold.

The sun in crystal amber on each limb
will disappear as spring begins its thaw.
Its diamond luster melts; a duller trim
of budding green is faceted in flaw.

And while the coming days grow long and soft
and vanquish memory of ice and frost,
I hear the winter's final winds aloft,
then silence, as its frozen voice is lost.

But mine remains in words that cling like rime
and whisper winter's beauty every time.

~

Spring

Allaire

Allaire, allow my heart to be your spring,
whose tree limbs bloom in tender green display,
inviting birds afar to nest and sing
their joyous songs upon an April day.

Allow, Allaire, my eyes to be your sun
that shines upon a land whose shadows fled
to yesterday, for winter's dark is done
and every dusk that dawns grows warm and red.

Allow this room to be your night's retreat,
where midnight's moans and moon are ever shared.
Allow my love to make your life complete,
and with your silent lips your trust declared.

Then, I will give my heart this spring to you,
and you'll allow your heart to love me too.

~

Behold The Spring

Behold the beauty of each springtime day,
whose roaming sun attracts the tender sky,
like you, my love, whose gaze had chanced my way
and stole my heart that once you caught my eye.

The growing softness of the greening hills
reminds me of your warm and supple skin.
The fullness of the landscape's bosom spills
within my grasp and then my mind within.

And every blade of grass my fingers seek
bends back in sweet surrender 'neath the air;
and nature's naked truth on vale and peak
is sprawled upon the earth for us to share.

Then God Himself will blanket spring's desire
with twilight warmth and stars He sets afire.

~

Don't Leave Yet, Spring

Don't leave yet, Spring; perhaps you'll pity me,
and green again this soil, grown bare and dry,
with tender grasses like a gentle sea,
upon whose surface floats each passerby.

Please paint the sky again; your azure blue
reminds me heaven is in full display.
The transient April showers passing through
are quite forgiven and not in the way.

But most of all, preserve each fragile leaf,
upon the hardy bough its life must cling...
It has no knowledge of the autumn grief
that comes too soon beyond your tenure, Spring.

Nor would I want to know such fate's at hand,
so fool me, too, and stay upon this land.

~

My Favorite Flower

My favorite flower in this fancy field
is not the one that's picked to primp your hair.
Its colorful corolla cannot yield
a face as beautiful as yours to share.

The distant hilltop flaunts its curvy rise
seducing skies to kiss its verdant crest.
Your figure lures me with supine surprise,
as we draw nearer when we stop to rest.

And in your eyes I see the spring's new sun;
and on your lips I taste such rosy red.
The Earth may still belong to everyone,
but God has given us His very bed.

Now, here, surrounded by each lovely bloom,
you're lovelier than all in nature's room.

~

Once the Spring...

I'm lost among the silly daffodils
that spring delivers with its yellowed smile.
Though once they cheered me, now their jaundice fills
the season's fields with blooms not worth the while.

When once the cherry blossoms blushed the sky
and painted Heaven's blue with perfect pink,
not nature's art, but spots and stains, see I,
like God's own poem blotched by curdled ink.

Not long ago, you loved me; I loved you...
Now daisies mock me as I shy away.
When you departed, you took springtime too;
left April's showers, yet no flowered May.

Yes, once the spring was more than spring could be;
you loved me not, and spring does not love me.

~

The Spring Snuck In

The spring snuck in before a second glance
was given to the winter, parting ways.
So much seems lost to cold and icy chance,
while tender grasses find emerging days.

The chill subsides; the sun is warm and high.
The trees are tickled green on branch and limb.
The sparrows sing again; their songs deny
the echoes of the world's more plaintive hymn.

And in the soil and sky we find our soul, —
in silly daffodils and butterflies
that dance to make our wounded spirit whole
and clear the fears that sometimes cloud our eyes.

Someday, we'll laugh at winter's worried worst,
and celebrate the spring's unyielding burst.

~

Woman of Spring

What woman — who? could steal these lines from me,
and stake her claim within this verse's heart,
to elevate it from mere poetry,
beyond the world of some fool's humble art?

Could it be you, whom I have cherished here?
Or you, who gazes so with starry eyes?
You? who, reading, sheds a lovelorn tear;
or you, who scorns the dawn for moonlight's rise?

I've given more than love, I've given time
beyond the grave and gravity of Earth.
I broke my heart for each eternal rhyme.
But, who? What woman is this sonnet's worth?

Yes, you! who woo yourselves, like darling birds
that sing of spring although they knew no words.

~

Summer

Common Ground

Behold the solstice when the sun is high,
and yet my heart has sunken well below
the far horizon of a fractured sky
that canopies the weary world in woe.

In black and white, the earth seems split in two:
this lonely beach, a buffer zone between
a sea, whose raging waves cannot break through
to land, whose brotherhood remains unseen.

And standing on this fragile, sandy strip, —
a billion fallen stars beneath my feet;
I neither move ashore nor take a dip,
but stay to suffer mankind's coldest heat.

Come meet me here, this day is never wrong;
we'll search for common ground all summer long.

~

How Soon July

How soon July descends upon the land,
its sun and moisture penetrate my skin,
like you, whose sultriness will take command,
whose heat then seeps into my heart within.

The scarlet waters flow upon this shore,
to saturate the sand beneath our feet;
and hand-in-hand we walk, then walk no more;
then sit, this ecru spot our only seat.

I turn to you, and you to me as well,
amid the rushing and receding sea;
and soon we both succumb to summer's spell.
And I to you and you as well to me.

Now, here we lay our souls beneath the sky,
our dreams the canopy; our bed, July.

~

I Miss the Moon

I miss the magic of the surging tide
that scattered twilight into glittered gold.
Those pristine jewels when earth and sea collide
are tarnished to a spirit, grown too old.

I miss the moon and miss the starry sky
that I had gazed upon each summer night,
before the cares of life would dull my eye
and obfuscate the heavens' silver light.

But most of all I miss our cherished beach,
its ecru satin on which we would dream
is empty now, its wonders out of reach,
and dark without my love's requited gleam.

The lustrous joys my heart held yesterday,
like shoreline driftwood are all swept away.

~

I Miss You, August

I miss you, August, and your sultry sun,
whose glow and heat will never hint of Fall;
unlike September's final week that, done,
will cast a shadowed chill upon us all.

Unlike July, whose overheated ways
usurp the gentler summer of sweet June,
my heart is held by August's steady days —
her season faithful and not leaving soon.

And then there's you, whose season always snows
and brings its feebler February light:
a pale reflection of what August shows
to me, alone with fonder dreams at night.

How once your beauty like the summer burned
with August's temperament before it turned.

~

I Search For August

I search for August in reluctant ways,
to find its heart amid its heat and light.
I study lonely clouds on sunny days
and stare the moon down on its jilted flight.

The blades of grass upon which I now lie
are softer than the bed where I had lain.
The trees above me seem depressed and cry,
but theirs are tears of joy from summer rain.

Then far afield awaits the golden shore,
the ocean shines with August's alchemy;
and yet such summer beauty casts no more
than darkness with its heartless sorcery.

You have no heart, cruel August, none I find;
and none had she when she left me behind.

~

Like Sun Through Summer Skies

I think of you and then I contemplate
the open beauty of the summer sky —
a sun that early dawns, while dusk comes late,
a spectral vista rendering each sigh.

A height that only Heaven could exceed,
beyond a blue, divine, as are your eyes,
where I'm held captive by this unknown need
to follow you like sun through summer skies

Too shy to gaze on you directly though,
I might as well a summer shadow be...
Too bright and beautiful to let you know,
you rise and set while never seeing me.

And when my night descends upon your day,
its tears are turned to stars your summer way.

~

September's Shore

Late summer's sunrise stirs the sleepy skies,
as ceding starlight slowly disappears.
Cicadas strain to sound their last good-byes,
while distant, breaking waves now greet my ears.

Each step upon September's shore is met
by sweet persuasion of the patient tide.
Its pull upon my feet is gentle, yet
invites me with a force that won't subside.

With carefree instinct, hungry seagulls drift
upon the thermals of the ocean's breath.
They hunt for breakfast, but I'd swear their lift
is more an angel's flight than perch for death.

In tranquil solitude this dawn, I pray
September's summer won't be swept away.

~

Summer Solitude

Alone, within a world of solitude
with nothing but the summer sky ahead,
where only pillowed clouds in flight protrude
from unseen hands onto an azure bed.

Below my feet, the sprawling meadow feels
as soft and satin as last evening's sheet.
The bosom of the distant hills reveals
the sultry Earth, undressed in August's heat.

And, still, I think of you; and, still, I see
your beauty in the beauty of this day.
I walk alone, but have your company —
in every path I find along the way.

And where the endless road leads out of sight…
there God must be, along with you tonight.

~

Summer's Edge

I know these trees upon the summer's edge,
when June's last day succumbs to sweet July
and my love sat upon the porch's ledge
to sing along as sparrows sung nearby.

The golden sun caressed her soft, pale cheek,
then set in crimson to reflect her blush.
At midnight, once again she'd sit to seek
the moon's cool silver, coating leaves and brush.

Within these woods, the hidden heartbeats sound —
their wounded stillness hums within my ear.
It called to her and, with a silent bound,
she left, and never would she reappear.

Now, summer, like my love, each season flees
among the shelter of the trusted trees.

~

The Gliding Gulls

The gliding gulls above September's sea,
whose wings in waves caress the lonely shore,
still skirt its turquoise carpet earnestly
in search of food, or love, who knows for sure?

I think of you while sitting on the sand,
imagine how your naked toes would trace
the vast horizon where there is no land
as I edge closer to your secret space.

And here beneath the endless midday sky,
I count each gull above the crested foam,
but not with numbers, with each lovelorn sigh,
and know my heart still seeks its perfect home.

If only you were lying by my side,
my dreams, not prayers, above these waves would glide.

~

The Naked Sun

Your beauty, I have not perceived before,
and, like the cosmos, cannot understand
why light, so heavenly, finds Earth's dark shore
or your eyes sparkle in this star-less land.

The Moon's a maiden, whose pale company
abandons lonely men in bed at night.
She lies to them with dreams that wane then flee;
I dream of you instead in stark daylight.

And in my dream, you are the naked Sun,
whose touch is soft with heat and golden glow;
whose smile commands the skies where rainbows run;
whose summer holds me and will not let go.

And what have I to make your own heart melt? —
perhaps, these words, whose fire I have felt.

~

The Summer, Lost

I've lost the summer, though the summer's green
is spread on every limb through leaves, revealed;
and in the sky to every eye is seen
a blue afire in God's sunny field.

Beyond, the fair horizon melts away
in hues of earthy tones and Heaven's tint;
and yet my world seems cold, its colors gray;
the sunrise sinks, the twilight has no glint.

Yet there we were upon an August shore,
once played in moonlight, silvering our skin.
Its evening sheen has dulled; I dream no more.
The full moon hides behind its waning grin.

Come back! Come back! September still has breath,
and summer lives until its autumn death.

~

Fall

All Love Is Gold

We want our love and love's gold light to stay
beyond the breaking dusk and rising eve,
and yet the waning Moon from Earth will stray,
the Sun from east to west will always leave.

The summer soon surrenders every limb,
once green and limber, to the autumn's chill,
which turns their soft-leafed beauty brown and dim,
to fall upon our feet at nature's will.

But one ought not forget the heart will store
in every living beat love's memory,
and what we think we've lost we'll find once more,
like spring, renewed from winter's barren tree.

Beyond the autumn's turning day and night,
there's you whose love remains a golden light.

~

Autumn's Heart

In every golden leaf, a life's betrayed,
for though its color boasts the autumn sun
one final time, its golden hue will fade
and fall upon the ground, its time soon done.

With every whisper carried from their trees,
the rustling leaves suspect their pending death.
I strain my ear upon the autumn breeze,
to hear God's voice, but only catch my breath.

And through these fractured limbs, the sun's gold eye
bears witness to a world that's torn apart.
Uncertainty tears up the empty sky;
can love exist if autumn has no heart?

Today, the hanging leaves deny despair;
tomorrow, golden silence stills the air.

~

Fall's Good-bye

Forever does your love in summer glow
and steals its fire from the sultry sky,
so even when its fleeting months must go
your heat remains with me, like mid-July.

Eternal is September's turning hour,
before the fall takes summer's breath away
like you, whose gentle lips my lips devour
then leave their whispers of this autumn day.

The summer can't be held for long, but you
can hold it here for me in every line;
and I, who tried to hold you longer, knew
no real embrace but this would make you mine.

And as I watch the greenest leaf turn gold,
still autumn can't break free of summer's hold.

~

September's Beauty

September's beauty comes at summer's end
before the deeper chill of rushing fall
will harden lush and limber leaves, to send
a warning whisper of the winter's call.

Before my heart succumbs to shorter days,
one golden moment more is all I seek,
for love is like the summer sun that stays
above us, hot and high and ours to keep.

Before the autumn's restless days are due,
I hope September's final week will tell
that, if I give my lovelorn heart to you,
no other month will speak for me as well.

So, darling, though the summer cannot stay,
September's beauty makes its final play.

Then September Came

You loved me once but then September came,
and summer's final days were soon at hand.
The breath of autumn breathed your chilly name,
and then the fall was spread across the land.

I looked for you between the falling leaves,
for though they drop, they drop in red and gold.
October's precious jewels my heart soon grieves,
their glitter can't fend off the coming cold.

Below the barren trees, I walk alone;
now tread upon their tarnished treasure, spread
beneath my feet in dull, diminished tone,
until each weighty step that proves them dead.

What once shone lofty in the azure sky,
like love, comes down to earth, then waits to die.

~

There's No More August

There's no more August; August's gone away
and left the shore of our sweet summer beach.
Yet, I remain, alone, a castaway;
and you have disappeared beyond my reach.

Beyond receding tides, September looms
and carries you upon its gentle wave,
until the longing in my heart resumes
and brings October storms that I must brave.

And how can I beyond this sandy strand
survive without your sultry company?
There's no more August on the sea or land,
and only Autumn's surge remains with me.

Come back, before this tempest can't be tamed,
or such a summer, we both knew, reclaimed.

~

We All Do Fade

We all do fade as does a leaf in fall,
whose green becomes the dusty brown of earth,
which, when so young, was lifted up so tall
upon the branch that bore its lofty birth.

We all do fall as does the sinless deer
that cannot understand the woodland yell
of hunters' victory to reach its ear
soon after dropping to its leafy Hell.

We all do die as does my own heart now,
for when I look upon each autumn tree,
I know that spring will resurrect each bough,
unsure if God will raise my destiny.

And when beneath that plot of leaves I'm laid,
please leaf through this, for this will never fade.

~

A Sonnet For All Seasons

Each Day Its Autumn Meets

How quickly does each day its autumn meet
and wither on the limb of time's cruel tree,
to fall like leaves, forgotten, at my feet,
then scatter in the winds of memory.

Too slowly does my heart through winter thaw
and beat with January's icy sun,
whose stolen fire can't inspire awe
from faithless gods, who their own heaven shun.

And spring, without you here, cannot return;
or summer saunter through our lovely park.
The sultry, midnight moon and stars won't burn;
the universe, like love, has lost its spark.

And time, cruel time, whose season, steady, stays,
will mock us for our fallen, forlorn days.

~

I Stand Alone

I stand alone upon this noble page
for all the world in unison to see;
each line below my feet is sound and sage,
and yet supports no audience but me.

With careful crafting, every word I write
becomes a tribute to each season's time.
The winter, summer, spring, and fall unite
in cold or sultry weather, set to rhyme.

Yet all a poet seeks at every turn,
through syllables that sound out from his sheet,
is that one distant heart he can discern
beyond the distance of his own heart beat.

Thus, whosoever sighs once this is through,
your whisper wills me on to write for you.

~

Summer Waves

I wonder if my words will last much more
than sunshine scattered on the summer waves,
which glisten magically until, ashore,
they rush and break upon their sandy graves...

like autumn leaves, whose vivid colors play
and dance in gentle breezes through each tree
until they're dulled and dried and blown away
and fallen in the fall's cold destiny.

And as I tread on winter's pristine snow
and feel its pureness pressed beneath my boot, —
I'm happy knowing spring has yet to grow
and bare the beauty of its tender shoot.

Yet here, then, does my heart impress its rhyme:
a page, and nothing more to last through time.

~

The Longer Shore

I walk the longer shore this August day,
and linger on its edge of sun and sea,
for soon September comes to take away
the summer that I thought belonged to me.

The ecru sand massages weary feet;
the ocean spray revives my open face.
What joy to live and feel such splendored heat
that none in other seasons can replace.

And you, who walks with me beneath the sun;
whose hand I reach for when the spring turned gold;
will you belong to me when summer's done,
and warm me through the fall and winter's cold?

No footsteps last upon this brief terrain,
and yet their imprints in my heart remain.

~

Your Sweet Addiction

The sweet addiction of your love is all
I need to carry me, both day and night,
through sultry summer's June, September's fall,
the dark of winter, and the spring's new light.

The sun needs only dawn to get so high;
the full moon finds its fix with midnight's rise.
Your gentle face is all I see, and I
want no withdrawal from your gazing eyes.

Had I one breath to breathe, I'd crave your kiss;
one final pulse, too weak, I'd draw you close
to feel your naked heart, so I'd not miss
the lasting beat of its undying dose.

A welcome drug are you, whose beauty flows
within my veins...and lines each reader knows.

~

BE MY VALENTINE...

No Love But Yours

In all my empty heart, no love but yours
has occupied each crimson corner so,
has coursed its passageways, seeped 'neath its doors,
then poured within with such a flooding flow.

No one but you completely claimed my heart,
restored the rhythm to its vacant beat.
You raised my pulse and made sweet music start —
your passion playing from my head to feet.

Now, here I am with pen and page at hand.
This ink, that runs like blood, can it be mine?
This page bears words that I don't understand;
I wrote them all for you, my Valentine.

And what you gave my heart, my heart gives you —
a love that beats in rhyme through time for two.

~

Of All the Hearts

Of all the hearts that beat beyond my own,
like distant waves that break upon the shore,
it's yours, whose rhythm casts a yearning tone,
that lures me in with its hypnotic score.

Of all the stars that pierce the winter sky
and fill the haunting hollow of its space,
none burns with brilliance to my gazing eye
as those sweet orbs that light your lovely face.

And when the moon reclines on midnight's bed,
and lies with me upon the evening's sheet,
I swear I feel your sultry softness spread,
like February touched by summer's heat.

Of all the beauty I could dream or view,
my heart and sight are blind to all but you.

~

Upon This Day

Upon this day, my heart must skip a beat —
a pause to ponder all my love for you.
The years have passed me by in swift retreat,
too few remain before they all are through.

And, yet, each memory, untouched by time,
still brings me to the moment we first met.
I stole a kiss; the feeling was sublime.
You stole my heart; I never knew regret.

Although this Valentine to you is late
and but a substitute for words, too weak,
I've not forgotten how you changed my fate
with tender, rosy lips and blushing cheek...

or how each day since then, you stilled my heart
between these moving lines that I impart.

~

Valentine Gift

What gift for my sweet love can I bestow
upon her heart, whose heart's already mine?
What more can I give her so she will know
that she's my one and only Valentine?

What more at dawn besides God's golden jewel
can I hold up to her expectant eye?
What more besides the full moon's carat, cool,
or starry fires faceting the sky?

What more, the heat and cold of loving you?
What more, a love that's better while it's worse?
For secret though we are, our love is true —
a diamond truly set in this rough verse.

What gift can I bestow, bestow again,
besides the universe within my pen?

~

Valentine's Season

The coldest month bestows the warmest day
upon our hearts, to surely emphasize
that love's impervious to winter's way —
its frozen landscapes lit by graying skies.

For love is more the dewy dawn of spring,
whose grassy shafts awake to sunlight's kiss,
whose morning meadows rise from soil to bring
the Earth's eruption to a blossomed bliss.

My love is you, a bloom that verse will bear
within its garden bed of loving rhyme;
and in the dead of winter, you'll be rare:
a rose before a rose's growing time.

Though winter never could the spring divine,
poor spring will never know my Valentine.

~

What Is A Valentine?

What is a Valentine...a thorny rose?
whose longest stem was trimmed for your frail hand,
whose clumsy head was plucked and primped to pose
like plastic, scarlet velvet on demand.

A box of chocolates with an ornate bow
whose contents advertise their calories?
A fancy dinner out, to let you know
that money spent still doesn't grow on trees?

Or best...a mushy, fabricated card
with rhymes pretending that they're poetry.
The nearby dollar store is such a bard...
Did I forget to sign it lovingly?

Perhaps, it's this, my Valentine, instead:
before your eyes, these lines were never read.

~

What Love But You

What love have I but you, my Valentine?
You're all the world my world is meant to be.
The winter glows in February's shine,—
with icy diamonds set in every tree.

The thousand stars that dot the endless night
are there for me to form a ring for you,
to place upon your finger, hands held tight,
to seal our fate in love, forever true.

But in the Moon I see you most of all;
its silver circle hugs the lonely sky...
A dance so slow with Earth, it seems to stall,
yet my heart races at your gazing eye.

And by the racing of your own heartbeat,
our universe stands still, and we're complete.

~

For Our Only Son...

My Son, Beyond (I)

My son, the truest gift you gave to me,
beyond the measure of my own life's worth,
was celebrating your sweet infancy,
beyond the miracle of your life's birth.

Beyond September's warmth, when you were born,
beyond the summer, bringing autumn's death,
how could I know one winter morn I'd mourn
as January froze your final breath?

Too brief, your nineteen years; too cruel, today —
beyond which I no longer see a spring,
whose season shines on earthly souls at play,
while yours has now departed, taken wing…

to Heaven, where your springtime waits for you,
and you, beyond, await your father, too.

~

I Lost My Son (II)

I lost my son one January, when
the winter morn revealed its coldest heart.
He breathed his final breath, lay still, and then
the time had come for us to both depart.

Within the frozen soil, we dug his grave,
a copper coffin, blessed, became his bed;
and to the bare and brittle Earth we gave
another ornate corpse to join the dead.

How dumbly birds do sing when spring arrives,
their season's songs of sun and Heaven sound
like church hymns played for all the hopeful lives,
who numbly pray for loved ones underground.

Beneath my feet, where lies each buried bone,
the cemetery grass smells sweet, now mown.

~

Our Fathers (III)

You'll always be the little boy I held
and carried off to bed each night. Asleep,
within my arms, against my heart, so swelled
with pride, you gave your life to me to keep.

You gave your cherub cheeks and funny nose,
your father's eyes and mother's silky hair,
your chubby fingers and your tiny toes,
your trust and innocence, your health and care.

You gave your childhood; adolescence, too;
but in the end, you gave to God your soul.
It wasn't for your parents' keep, yet you,
in your short life, gave more than lives lived whole.

Yes, you will always be my little boy,
whom He now puts to sleep and holds with joy.

~

Good Sons (IV)

I'd give my life if I could give yours back,
uproot you from the grave in which you lie;
restore the color to the clothes of black
your mother wears to shadow her good-bye.

Though God returned the Virgin Mother's son,
to give to man a second chance to live,
what grief she must have felt when day was done,
to see men seek new sins He won't forgive.

So, stay, my son, and let your spirit rest,
and I will tend to mother's tearful pain.
Where you lie now in dirt and wood is blessed,
and Heaven won't give up good sons again.

From paradise, no one should be returned,
and yours, my son, has been forever earned.

~

Sunday Night (V)

Come Monday morning, mourning angers me:
Another week begins that we're without
the son whose life we made, whose destiny
was ours to oversee and care about.

Why would He take you at so young an age
and leave me to reflect this Sunday night?
Against the dying of the light men rage,
yet you, my son, so soon took silent flight...

So rage, now, son! Yes, rage upon your cloud!
God has enough bright souls and suns above;
for you were born to both your parents, proud,
and He and Heaven can't outshine our love.

And when this prayer is never answered, I
will rage each night with you, until I die.

~

Good Night, Sweet Son (VI)

Good night, sweet son, your sun has set to stay
and cannot rise in eyes that now are closed,
while mine, still open, open on this day
that stills my heart at your young heart reposed.

Good night, dear child; a child you'll always be
to mom and dad, — poor dad, who writes this scrawl
had prayed to God, God knows, religiously,
to spare your life and yet your life would fall.

Good night, good night, no night should be like this:
no dream to dream, no dawn can dawn anew;
and now I kneel, kneel down for one last kiss
to wake my soul, as we all wake yours too.

In death, perhaps, we'll find our final light.
Sweet dreams, sweet son, sweet dreams. Good night. Good night.

Spring's Green Joy (VII)

This afternoon, the season's rains arrive,
and spring begins anew with newer tears —
for you are dead, my son, and I'm alive;
the winter took from us your budding years.

It froze my heart, yet kept it beating still, —
preserved, like living things that hibernate;
but as life wakes, I've not the waking will
to wake with it and springtime celebrate.

O, look: a daffodil! And there: a rose!
On branch and bough, both bare, blooms verdancy!
But sorrow seeds my heart and grief thus grows
where spring's green joy cannot return to me.

Each flower risen in the spring, unchanged,
looks different now upon your grave, arranged.

~

Unknown Tears (VIII)

I live each moment like your final breath —
a soundless sigh that was your last goodbye —
I thought I heard you call my name at death,
but, no, you lay in silence there to die.

I thought your final shudder shed pain's shame,
absolving you from man's mortality;
I thought, again, my son, you called my name,
but, no, you passed to Heaven quietly.

One final time, before our time was done,
I poised my lips above your slumbered ears.
I thought I cried your name, my son! my son!
and hoped you heard me through such unknown tears.

Now this, forever, calls to you, beyond,
and all who read, my son, hear you respond.

~

His Eternity (IX)

You're Heaven's now in His eternity...
No matter how long I have left to live,
I'll grant you what you lost through poetry —
for what He's taken, I shall now re-give.

Behind the fabled gates of His domain,
do candied clouds and sugared saints hold true?
You're my sweet child; you should not there remain —
when Earth's true paradise was real for you.

No death shall keep you from your father's pen.
No God shall keep you penned against your will.
Return to us and be our son again,
and I will write your poems ever, still.

And each day through each word and through each line,
the world will know my love is more divine.

~

Beyond Your Death (X)

Beyond your death, dear child, does death deceive
your father's faith in God, who took my son;
and does He now rejoice, while I now grieve
without my little boy, my only one?

What of the joy your birth had given us?
A baby boy seemed God's own gift to send
to mom, whose years of nurturing and fuss
were blessed, then cursed, when your brief life would end.

I hope that Heaven is a haven, true,—
a better place for one's eternity;
but, still, too young, my son, too young were you,
and old, too old, have grown your mom and me.

Within your empty bedroom since, I search
for God's good truth...my heart, an empty church.

~

You're Gone, My Son (XI)

You're gone, my son, but not forgotten — no;
for as I walk among the solemn trees,
I see you in the twilight's gentle glow
and feel you in the summer's tender breeze.

With measured steps, I walk this grassy lane,
whose well-trimmed softness comforts foot and soul;
yet as my heart recalls last winter's pain,
I stop and sit beneath your nearby bole.

My son, we picked this spot for you to stay —
a piece of Heaven made of earth and sky;
and both your parents did their best and pray
that God Himself for this sweet spot would die.

Though, now, eternity reclaims you, son,
I too will lie with you when my day's done.

~

Your Father First (XII)

I am your father first, then He, my son,
your father who'd have given his life to
have spared you from His pearly gates, for none
at nineteen years of age should die like you.

Then, what a test of faith I'm left to brave —
yes, I, an orphaned soul of fatherhood —
for what good God would not his own Son save
from painful sacrifice to nail and wood.

So, son, this verse has now become my cross;
my feet are hung upon each line's detail;
my hands, forever moved by my heart's loss,
are pinned to this sheet's wood by this pen's nail.

All those who witness this ink's Calvary,
know I'm your father first, then second He.

You Died Too Soon (XIII)

You died too soon, and left me asking why
there can't be permanence through day and night.
The stars and sun, once fixed upon the sky,
look down on me with lost, unsettled light.

Each season quickly comes, more quickly goes;
the sun abandons summer. Leaf-filled trees,
once lush with tender life, flee autumn's throes
and run their course before the winter's freeze.

Yet, spring again arrives, its verdancy
breaks ground with innocence and vital need;
and though each flower's fate is known, won't we
still nurture it to bloom from infant seed?

Do Heaven's stars shine bright, its summer stay?
God took you, son, but can't take you away.

~

The Sycamore (XIV)

I miss you, son, and when the autumn leaves
are falling from these branches, think of you,
and wonder if the sycamore bereaves
its emptiness as I, now empty, do.

It stands unquestioning when winter's frost
arrives to coat each bare limb 'neath the sky.
The sycamore — does it feel all it's lost
as I, who witness every lone leaf die?

But God must pity more the sycamore,
re-buds its open arms each spring in May;
while my arms leave as empty as before,
and my heart emptier at His display.

Unlike the sycamore, so faithful, brave,
your father folds his arms above your grave.

~

Just The Sky (XV)

Should I in silence lay my head, be still,
above you, 'neath our weeping willow tree...
not hear the echoes of the whippoorwill
whose plaintive music seems to play for me.

...not see a canopy of fractured dreams
that mottles daylight's each true green and blue,
and though the bright sun through its branches streams,
so do deep shadows fall upon me too.

But I refuse to see this place as sad,
refuse not lie upon this shady ground;
refuse not keep you company. Your dad
delights each day in every sight and sound.

And I pray, son, that you look up, as I,
and know that Heaven's more than just the sky.

~

Sanctum (XVI)

Dear God, can you fill in this emptiness
as does his coffin fill this hallowed hole,
which days before was soil, nor more or less,
but now is sanctum for my son's poor soul?

Can you disguise these tears as winter rain
that streaks my face in January's chill
and falls to freeze upon this bleak terrain
as do my knees before my vanquished will?

And can you let me see that there is more
above this earth than just a graying sky?
Yes, more to paradise than just this floor
of worms and buried bones where loved ones lie?

Dear God, I'd give myself if you would raise
my child, whom I had raised in long-dead days.

~

This Lovely Day (XVII)

The heart cannot hold on to sadness long,
like sycamores, whose tender leaves will meet
their deaths in arms that sway to windy song
that swoons them for their fall at autumn's feet.

It can't hold on for long, like winter's spells
of ice that coat each plot of bare terrain.
Beneath each frozen surface spring still dwells,
and brings a tender soil to Earth again.

And you, whose tombstone, laid on soft, green grass
that rises from your grave so summery,
should know your father's days one day will pass
and I will join you underneath this tree.

For now, dear son, though I must walk away,
my heart holds on to you this lovely day.

~

My Penance (XVIII)

My penance, since your death, are splendored days
that soak my senses, while my heart won't share
in spring's deliverance of Heaven's rays
that bathe the Earth in God's own gilded air.

My purgatory is the summer scent
of lusty rose, its fragrance hot and strong,
yet placed upon your grave, its perfume spent, —
its scarlet soul succumbs before too long.

But no damnation curses me like fall,
whose magic turns green leaves to red and gold,
whose autumn alchemy can't fate forestall —
I watch once tender lives drop dead and cold.

Now, only winter's hellish truth looks right:
its snowy shroud laid out in lifeless white.

~

The Sycamores (XIX)

You left, dear son, as January came,
announcing nothing on its wintry wind, —
not bitterness or blasphemy or blame
or innuendo that your father sinned.

It settled silently and took its hold,
then filled the empty limbs of every tree
with untouched timelessness and ancient cold.
Yes! January came to you and me.

But, now, a whisper never heard before,
accuses me from up above, and I
stare guiltily at every sycamore,
whose trembling, bony branches brace the sky.

And you, whose soul to God your loved ones gave,
forgive your father's doubts above your grave.

~

We Search For Summer (XX)

We search for summer in the summertime
'midst hot July and August's fleeting stay,
and yet the summer seems much more sublime
when late September steals its final day.

How true, we cherish what we quickly grieve —
a sun that, high and gold, begins to wane,
a tree, whose verdant leaves begin to leave
and cede their tender souls to autumn's reign.

But you, dear son, laid 'neath the open sky
no longer watch each season pass nor spend
a worried thought that life has passed you by,
for your new summer's come and will not end...

And mine will stay upon this leaf of white,
and know no Fall by hands that hold it tight.

Dust and Destiny (XXI)

What comes to us but dust and destiny,
when years we've spent together fade away?
They dangled like the leaves on autumn's tree,
then died, then dropped, then still and silent lay.

That field, now empty, where you played is green;
the sky above it peaks in azure light.
I walk among old stones, 'til yours is seen,
as though it rises to His hallowed height.

October's prayers are dreams that never flew
nor reached their rainbow's end to happiness;
instead, they're grounded in the truth of you,
who hears the dirt of what my lips confess:

O, son, I've looked for you, but found no sign
beyond this plot that one day will be mine.

~

Sunday At St. Charles (XXII)

Dear daddy, let not dirt and gravest dust
weigh down the beauty of our Father's Day.
For in the end, it's always God we trust,
though His is such an odd, unknowing way.

Dear son, let not your tombstone be the card
that greets me like your childhood poems had,
for Rest In Peace befits no youthful bard,
whose cherished words would end: I Love You, Dad.

And let not gray upon this blue sky break;
or brittle brown the the soft, green grass soon grow.
The loveliness of spring will not forsake
a man, whose spirit does the winter know.

This perfect, Sunday morning I am blessed
with both my son and father, laid to rest.

Before My Sun Must Set (XXIII)

My worries seem a bit absurd right now,
for I still rise each day and see the sun;
its golden pleasure cascades through each bough
and spills upon the ground to you, dear son.

I step above the earth, you lie below.
Had I a whim, I could go anywhere.
Much summer's left, and yet my feet won't go:
I keep returning to this ground, right here.

And soon the autumn will turn leaves to gold;
they'll fall upon my heart in withered brown.
But you'll stay young each year, while I'll grow old;
and you look up to Him, while I'll look down.

Yes, teach me, son, to be much more like you,
before my sun must set and night seeps through.

~

December's Joy (XXIV)

My doleful heart adorns December's sky
and casts its somber shadow overhead.
Where once an ornamental sun blazed high,
a steely star of gray is set instead.

Where once the season's tree limbs blinked with lights
as festive as the faith that hung them there,
December's doubt burns steadily through nights
when silence answers questions, posed as prayer.

And somewhere deep beneath December's dust,
true joy is buried well below my feet,
which walk upon this frozen surface, just
to find the reason for my next heart beat.

Dear son, December shines with Christmastime
for most; for me, its spirit haunts this rhyme.

~

MONTHS...

January

Why comes the winter with its bitter winds,
its drifts of snow and ice that run too deep,
as though the earth the summer's warmth rescinds
and kills the rose we tried past June to keep?

Why does the gentle sparrow flee the spare
and brittle boughs for warmer southern climes,
yet I remain on pages, white and bare,
until this January greens in rhymes?

For there's no winter to a weathered heart,
whose beat has blossomed to love's blush, then lost
its rosy rhythm when love falls apart,
like flowers, petrified by dirty frost.

Amid the dead of winter, we will thrive
through words that flourish here, our love alive.

February

O, February, you, whose heart won't yield
to winter's cruel and cold and empty air,—
your boughs, thus, raised, your naked bark revealed,—
beseech some godly grace in rigid prayer.

I walk upon this ground and pass you by,
no roots like yours that run to depths below,
and peer into the same uncertain sky,
amazed that faith can keep you anchored so.

You bear the brunt of every testing storm;
you stand alone in upright dignity;
yet never flinch until sweet sparrows swarm
in spring to sing upon their favorite tree.

Were I as steady and as still as you,
there'd be no winter that I'd not pull through.

~

March

O, hardy March, you've braved the weather's worst,
withstood each tempest's fit for days on end,
and you, storm-tested, greet the springtime first,
are kissed by sparrows, who, in song, descend.

Small buds upon bare bark, like goosebumps, rise
and warm the skin of each sweet sycamore,
which longed for greener clothes in spring's new size,
to shed the snowy garb they sadly wore.

Although a wayward winter wind may try
once more to moan among your darling trees,
the spring's now ready with its own reply
of whispered comfort, blown in every breeze.

A final shiver of your limbs dispels
the winter's claim to where the spring now dwells.

~

April

Behold the smile that April mornings wear
through giddy daffodils, which yearly wake
and raise their golden noses in the air
to breathe a season in that God must make.

Through every blade of grass how green grow days,
when youth is everything, — immortal, blessed;
and on the altar of the springtime prays
each tree, whose lifted limbs on Heaven rest.

Then, children, running, legs in wanton stride,
young lovers, arm-in-arm, and hearts in sync
move poets, reaching for old pens, thought dried,
to resurrect their dreams in timeless ink.

And even I, with weary feet, pursue
that April dawn, once dawned for me and you.

~

May

O, May, O, May, you blossom buds on boughs
and decorate the skin of darling limbs.
You fill the air with song as sparrows rouse
my senses to their sweet and lofty hymns.

Above these branches, Heaven's dome soars high,
and blue infinity spans overhead.
Within the chapel of the open sky,
my heart to hers and hers to mine were wed.

No witness but the Sun, who gazed afield;
no rings exchanged, but those within this tree, —
love was confessed, yet our two lips were sealed,
and even God would guard its secrecy.

Then, this alone now documents that May.
Come back, my Love, and love me for today.

~

June

The early rose of June enjoined my heart;
its pieces, scattered, at last summer's end, —
like petals, soft to touch, yet pulled apart
by hands too harsh to be such beauty's friend.

The perfumed velvet of its scarlet head
enthralled my senses, tempted me to taste
the pleasures of each fluid fold, so red,
like her wet lips I drank in thirsty haste.

And yet the thorn of sweet desire tricked
my mind to think that love would also bloom.
Alas, my foolish heart was plucked and pricked
and felt the stab of her seductive doom.

Upon the stem of summer, June's new rose
for romance opens; with regret will close.

~

July

July, July, its summer heart will beat
with pounding waves upon a secret shore,
where you and I in stolen moments meet
and lie together on its sandy floor.

July, it stares at us with summer's eye,
whose sultry gaze undresses guilty care
that, cloaked in clouds that clothed a wintry sky,
is stripped beneath more hot and humid air.

July is sweltering; July is wet,
yet cools me with its salty ocean mist,
like she, whose steamy lips I'll not forget
as mine, with cold, departing ease, are kissed.

Good-bye, July; July, good-bye, for she,
like summer, drowned me in her torrid sea.

~

August

When August's final days have washed ashore
and stranded helpless creatures on the beach,
how sad that summer soon will be no more
and all our summer dreams are out of reach.

So, as I dig my feet into the sand
and dare the ancient tide take me away
to colder seasons and some unknown land,
I realize happiness this August day.

Here, you once walked with me beneath the sun,
collected seashells, bleached in Heaven's white.
I've kept them safely, treasuring each one
that sacrificed its life for your delight.

One day my August day, like yours, will die,
but this will drift to every hand and eye.

~

September

September rises with the summer sun
and, naked, dips into the glinting sea,
her beauty bared once more to everyone
before its clad in cooler modesty.

By afternoon, she walks through woods, whose leaves
still hold the summer's passion, lush and green.
Then, further on, September soon perceives
a change is coming to the season's scene.

September rests upon the earthy floor,
remembering the heat of mid-July,
reliving lusty dreams on August's shore,
and falls asleep beneath the dusky sky.

While stars align above her slumbered head,
when next she wakes, she wakes in autumn's bed.

~

October

October burns upon my heart in blue,
and fires up her sun in azure light,
her Hunter's Moon falls prey to Heaven's hue, —
a heathen stalked at God's own hallowed height.

October gilds the day in leaves of gold,
bejewels the evening with her starry sky.
Though leaves will fall and stars fade out when old,
their beauty ever shimmers in my eye.

Thus, I once fell for you when fall had burned,
then wished for you upon those blazing stars;
had filled my heart with gold, but you returned
my open arms with autumn's tarnished scars.

Now, as I walk beneath each turning tree,
October's wounded limbs reach out to me.

~

November

November never knows a leaf to stay
upon its bough in joyous, gentle green
or golden in the fall's most perfect day.
Her trees are dull and all their branches lean.

Her bed's made up, a final resting place
for springtime memories of limber limbs
that flourished in the summer's sultry grace,
then aged so gracefully in autumn's trims.

And as November dresses down to sleep,
I lie with her beneath the chilly sky
and daydream of a spring we could not keep,
whose warmest memory will never die.

Through every rustling leaf that nestles near,
November's sweetest-nothings fill my ear.

~

December

December sashays into Winter's arms
on feet, unburdened by the Fall's dead weight;
and thus embraced, she's swooned by Winter's charms —
his icy calm and cool, collected gait.

She decorates her home in warm regard
to holidays, inviting Winter in.
Still, he remains reserved, his heart too hard,
but she, too lonely, bares her pallid skin.

While rising from her bed, he turns to her
and bends to kiss December's gentle cheek.
Then she, in slumber, utters only Brrr.
As he departs, the floor boards, brittle, creak.

On Christmas morn, December wakes and finds
the Winter's gift of snow outside her blinds.

~

For My Wife, My Only One...

A Million Years Ago (I)

I married you a million years ago,
and nothing since has ever been the same.
You stole my heart and never let it go;
and gave up yours, as well as your last name.

I still remember that first awkward kiss,
as though our lips could somehow calm our nerves.
You shut your eyes and hoped I would not miss,
but love is blind and finds what it deserves.

And in that breathless moment time stood still;
and no one else existed in that space.
The sun and moon and stars could never fill
my universe as would your sweetest face.

From then to now a million years have passed;
or maybe none, our kiss still holds me fast.

~

The You I Had (II)

I always thought we'd have more time to spend
beneath these autumn skies, so crisp and blue.
But fate stepped in to make October send
each falling leaf without its colored hue.

For forty years, our lives were intertwined;
our hearts beat daily as though they were one.
How could our union not be God-divined?
Why would He now decide that it was done?

And so I'm pondering: why you, not me...
Is loneliness the penance now I face?
Or am I here to make sure others see
The you I knew and never will replace?

Through these mere words, like leaves that autumns blow,
you'll spread through time and in each heart will grow.

~

The Best Bouquet (III)

The best bouquet I ever gave to you
is now the one I gently place to stay
beneath an empty sky's November blue,
upon the ground, both green and grave today.

Its fresh-cut petals glow with guilty glee,
too bright and cheerful to show true respect.
And so I bow my head more solemnly,
and force myself to be as circumspect.

But your loss doesn't flash before my eyes;
I feel instead the sun's warmth on my skin;
and then your fingers too... To my surprise,
they touch my heart as though they reach within.

Now on this unexpected plot, I stand
and clasp the sun as though it were your hand.

~

It's Been Two Months (IV)

It's been two months since you had passed away,
and Christmastime will never be the same.
The tree's still stored and that's where it shall stay;
there's no new gift to place with your sweet name.

The lights outside still blink in mocking cheer.
I ponder why the neighbors hang them so.
She's gone, you fools! I wish they'd disappear..."
But I can't blame them, even if they know.

I wander outside while I wonder, lost,
and cannot celebrate the season's joy,
like children ceding Santa at the cost
of finding no more magic in each toy.

My Christmas present waking up this morn
was always you, not He, for being born.

~

Whenever Night Prevails (V)

I miss you most whenever night prevails,
and, weary, I succumb to lay my head
upon this pillow left, but still it fails
to bring me comfort without you in bed.

The winter's blanket is no substitute,
although you picked its fabric and its tone.
Without you underneath, its warmth is moot:
its cover covers me in cold, alone.

But worse, I dread the morning's eager rise
that lifts me from this room to start anew.
There's no more you: no smile, no big brown eyes;
yet still I wake to see each day's end through...

Until the evening calls me back to sleep,
and sends me dreams of you I try to keep.

~

What Spring Is There? (VI)

What spring is there to love when you are not?
The season's gray, not filled with greenery;
the clouds still hover, for the sun forgot
to fill the sky with sunny scenery.

The sparrow sings, but who can hear his tune?
The roses bud, but I won't smell their bloom.
The dusk delivers night without a moon;
the night delivers me a dreamless room.

And should I, restless, kneel before this bed
to pray that spring return once more to me,
or lie right here and let my winter spread
like icy darkness through eternity?

Wherever spring has gone, it's gone to stay;
perhaps, I'll find it on my dying day.

~

I Hear Your Whisper (VII)

I hear your whisper from a distant place,
whose sight is out of reach to me right now;
and such a gentle breath upon my face
reclaims me with your love and endless vow.

You'll find someone. Yes, give it time, they say.
Yet timeless was the bond we forged through rings.
You left me, but you'll never go away.
Hang tight! You'll see who else tomorrow brings.

But love was not dispensed with when you died,
nor is an energy that is conserved.
It's held within me, buried deep inside, —
for no one else...no matter how deserved.

It's you whose heart, though stilled, still stills my own;
its echoes haunt me now that I'm alone.

~

We Danced But Once (VIII)

We danced but once, upon our wedding day;
your feet were clumsy and my own much more.
We wouldn't have it any other way,
for our hearts floated on that magic floor.

We celebrated our new fate to come...
a champagne toast to kick off this sweet life.
My mother cried, your father smiled, and, dumb,
I felt immortal holding my young wife.

Too soon, I danced with you down Jesus' aisle;
and always shy, you mutely acquiesced.
This time, the band played more in organ style,
its music meant to lift those laid to rest.

We're gathered here, my once beloved and I,
whom God had joined, though knowing one would die.

~

August Dream (IX)

I dream of August and our holding hands,
while walking on the beach with you alone.
The sun kilns both the sky and stepped-on sands
to mix earth's summer blue with ecru bone.

Its golden eye above dismisses us,
a couple trapped in life's mortality;
and who goes first is not what we discuss,
or when things end in this reality.

But one may pass and leave the other here
to retrace footsteps on a lonely shore.
I push aside this thought and hold you near,
enjoy our time, and think of it no more...

Until I wake without you by my side,
a petty seashell stranded by the tide.

~

Widower Warrior (X)

I wear the badge of widower so well —
a warrior who's fought off timely tears —
for through each turn of grief, I didn't dwell
on sudden sadness, just our happy years.

I dug a trench into my silty soul,
and jumped right in without a bayonet.
With only my heart bared in this foxhole,
I held back every guilt and each regret.

And, thus, when I emerged, the battle done,
and stood upon the lip of victory,
it's you I still will miss...What have I won
but just another day of only me?

A victor, who surrenders now to rhyme
the love he shared with you in life's brief time.

~

Back To Berlin (OH) (XI)

We never took that Amish buggy ride
like simple folk whose courtship's on display
for all the tourists through the countryside
who wish simplicity were their own way.

Without a canopy, their hearts reveal
the blushed restraint upon each other's face;
and then his hands reach for her own to feel
the thrilling softness of her modest grace.

Back! Back! to sweet Berlin, where we had known
a love that forty years ago was pure.
Since then you've passed, and now I drive alone
to see if sweethearts ride and still endure.

When morning comes, my horseless carriage, fleet,
departs with your love in an empty seat.

~

Her Final Gift...

Little Gifts (XII)

She asked for little gifts that year from me, —
and twelve in total to be picked with care,
to place beneath our special Christmas tree...
our first as newlyweds; our first to share.

I made a list, and checked it more than twice.
I struggled both with time and what love brings.
I wrote down something naughty, something nice;
and tried my best to find her twelve small things.

Alas, by one, I'd fallen short that morn.
All twelve from her were there: she didn't miss.
Then, she just laughed to know my heart was torn,
and healed it with her Christmas morning kiss.

And that was all the gift she really sought, —
my love for her, not little things I bought.

~

About The Author

M.D. Petti is a hopeless romantic, whose Brooklyn, NY upbringing helps to ground him in reality. He is the author of two previously published poem-novels, *Sweet Jen* and *KIS:S*, and two books of poetry, *Discovered World* and *Seasons & Sonnets* (both with Minerva Bloom).

He currently lives in Lititz, PA with his daughter and their golden retriever, Ripley, and Japanese Chin, Mika.

www.ingramcontent.com/pod-product-compliance
Lightning Source LLC
Chambersburg PA
CBHW062048080426
42734CB00012B/2591